GW00320448

San Francisco

Berlitz Publishing Company, Inc.
Princeton   Mexico City   Dublin   Eschborn   Singapore

Text:	Paula Tevis
Editor:	Media Content Marketing, Inc.
Photography:	Chris Coe except pages 3, 4, 6, 64, 68, 76, 98 by Doug Traverso
Cover Photo:	Chris Coe
Photo Editor:	Naomi Zinn
Layout:	Media Content Marketing, Inc.
Cartography:	Ortelius Design

Although the publisher tries to insure the accuracy of all the information in this book, changes are inevitable and errors may result. The publisher cannot be responsible for any resulting loss, inconvenience, or injury. If you find an error in this guide, please let the editors know by writing to Berlitz Publishing Company, 400 Alexander Park, Princeton, NJ 08540-6306.

ISBN 2-8315-7706-3

Printed in Italy
010/008 REV

CONTENTS

• A 🖝 in the text denotes a highly recommended sight

San Francisco

THE CITY AND ITS PEOPLE

Earthquakes aside, there's just no shaking off San Francisco. One of America's favorite cities, San Francisco clings to your soul, as irresistibly as a yen for the good things in life, or a song that won't vacate your head. The ballad may be syrupy, but so many millions of people have left their hearts in San Francisco that you can't fight it: The City by the Bay incites love at first sight — a love that lasts.

The first astonishment is the setting. So many thrillers have been filmed in San Francisco that the hills look as familiar as home; and yet it turns out that the cameramen didn't need trick lenses; the hills are just as giddily steep as in the movies. Officially, 43 hills stand up to be counted, most famously Nob, Russian, Telegraph, and Twin Peaks. From these vantage points the views are endlessly varied and stimulating — the magnificent Pacific, the choppy bay and its mysterious islands, and other hills dotted with mansions, eccentric Victorian houses, or skyscrapers with character. And if somewhere in the world there is a more noble bridge than the Golden Gate, its glory isn't crowned with wisps of fog.

The sound of a foghorn is as much a San Francisco particular as the clang of a cable car bell. First heard in the 1870s, that bell still incites the squeals of tourists hanging on as the cable car rounds a bend. More subtly, you can hear the actual cable speeding under the street at a relentless 9 1/2 mph (15 km/h), perpetually protesting like a distant alarm clock. A more piercing aural trademark is the tweet of the tin whistle of a hotel doorman commanding a taxi in the sunshine, or pleading for one in the drizzle. In ethnic neighborhoods the sounds are as exotic as the hiss of a North Beach espresso machine or the slurping of soba noodles in Japantown.

Even in summer — more so in summer, when much of California is broiling — the San Francisco weather is invigorating. Thanks to a temperate marine climate, as it's called, the mercury rarely tops 70°F (21°C) at any time of year. Thus, except for the more arduous hills, which are best tackled by cable car or bus, San Francisco is definitely a city for walkers. How else could you appreciate the architectural adventure of the high skyscrapers in the Financial District, the abundance of Italian cafés in North Beach, or the pungent aromas of Chinatown?

San Francisco has always been a melting pot, especially since international fortune-hunters flooded in to exploit the gold rush of the mid-19th century. At the moment, the largest single ethnic group in the city is Chinese, though every culture in the world seems to be represented, as evidenced by the mushrooming roster of ethnic restaurants, from Afghani to Vietnamese.

Home-grown Americans from all parts of the country keep moving in, attracted by the scenery, the eternal springtime, and a truly cosmopolitan atmosphere in a city of fewer than three-quarters of a million people. Another intangible inducement is a very civilized tolerance. San Francisco respects its minorities of all stripes, including starving artists, splinter-party politicians, and militant homosexuals.

All this is going on in a relatively compact corner of the West Coast, the tip of the peninsula. It is here that the city and county of San Francisco, which coincide, cover about 46 square miles (120 sq. km) — one-tenth of the area of Los Angeles. To put San Francisco into a more metropolitan context, the region is considered to include Oakland, San Jose, and the rest of the nine-county Bay Area, totaling 6 million people. Even so, the resident population is outnumbered by the annual tourist influx by a ratio of more than two to one.

San Francisco Bay, a naval, commercial, and recreational haven of 496 square miles (1,285 sq. km), went undiscovered until rather late in the colonization of America. For a couple of centuries, Spanish, Portuguese, and English sailors must have sailed on past the Golden Gate, where the Pacific meets the bay, but it seems to have been fogbound every time. Finally, in 1769, the Spanish pioneer Gaspar de Portolá exclaimed over a harbor big enough to shelter all the navies of Europe. It was a sort of backdoor discovery, for his party stumbled on the bay from land, not sea. Seven years later Spanish colonists arrived and set up a fort to defend the bay, and built a mission to convert the local Native Americans. Mission Dolores, which is still here, was dedicated to St. Francis of Assisi, or, as they say in Spanish, San Francisco.

San Francisco caters well to its many visitors, and there are lots of ways to see the sights.

By 1846, when the town, then ruled by Mexico, was claimed by the United States, there was nothing much to brag about — a trading post with fewer than a thousand inhabitants. Two years later, a revolution was sparked by a four-letter word: gold. The bonanza on the American River, 140 miles (225 km) away, catapulted San Francisco to the status of an international dream. And there was no looking back. The Barbary Coast was eventually tamed, but the idea of a land of limitless opportunity still persisted. Even today, with omnipresent panhandlers reminding tourists of grim contemporary social problems, an overriding optimism wafts in with the tangy Pacific breeze.

The threat of earthquakes is all too real for the people of San Francisco, as everyone was tragically reminded in 1989, when the city trembled at a shrug of the San Andreas Fault. Seismological phenomena are a fact of life in California, where some people wait for the Big One with the fatalism of a fisherman in a typhoon.

The earthquake of October 1989, shown "live" on television from Candlestick (3Com) Park during the baseball World Series, was far less terrible than the catastrophe of 1906 that became the great dividing line in San Francisco's history. On

that occasion hundreds of men, women, and children lost their lives, fires burned for three days, and the city was all but wiped out.

Many hundreds of Victorian landmarks were preserved or restored, but what replaced the rubble was an elegant 20th-century city, worthy of its position as unofficial capital of the American West. (Los Angeles has since overtaken San Francisco in population and power,

Nothing says San Francisco quite like its extravagant Victorian homes.

Ferries come and go at busy Pier 39, taking passengers to Alcatraz and/or around the bay for a famous view or two.

although, according to most visitors, L.A. offers little competition when it comes to charm.) Culture is thriving in San Francisco, with its opera, symphony orchestra, ballet, theaters, museums, and universities, and spills over into the areas of refined shopping and eating.

Like its setting and its history, San Francisco is romantic, but with so much to see and do, the pace can become hectic. For relief, cross the bay to the heavenly sanctuary of the redwoods, the sunny valleys of vineyards, or waterside villages that seem more Mediterranean than Californian. On the return journey, soak up the mood of the harbor, its islands, sailboats, and ferries, and the San Francisco skyline, a thrilling clash of high-rise majesty, low-slung homes, and sprinkles of parkland. If there were nothing here but 43 bare hills, it would still be a marvel.

A BRIEF HISTORY

Until the American Revolution, the San Francisco Bay Area, isolated by ocean and mountains, languished in prehistoric obscurity. While 18th-century Bostonians were going to Harvard, humming the catchy music of the young Mozart, the inhabitants of this region were fishing and trapping. They were Indians of the Ohlone (or Costanoan) tribe, so far removed from modern influences that they had never seen a horse or a wheel.

Not until 1776 did the first colonists — the Spanish — arrive at what is now San Francisco, where they built a presidio, or military garrison, and a religious mission to convert and educate the Indians. Settlement began seven years after the first Europeans had discovered the mighty bay. Ships from many European nations, sailing up and down the Pacific coast, had been missing the Golden Gate for centuries, probably because of the fog. The best-known explorer to come close was Sir Francis Drake, who is said to have landed farther north in 1579 at what is now Drake's Bay. He claimed everything in sight for England, but nobody took any notice.

In the early years the Spanish colony showed no particular promise. The Presidio, overlooking the Golden Gate, was never called on to repel invaders, and so unimpressive were the defenses that the commander was reprimanded during the late 1700s when he twice entertained the captain of a visiting British Royal Navy ship, thus disclosing his unpreparedness.

Meanwhile, inland, the mission went about its evangelical work, but many Indians died before they could be forced to convert, as European diseases rampaged through their population.

Mexicans and Gringos

California came under Mexican control in 1821, when Mexico won its independence from Spain. A few years later the new regime secularized the network of California missions, including Mission Dolores. The church's extensive lands were reassigned to settlers, some of whom amassed huge cattle ranches. With the Franciscan friars out of a job, the native Indians tragically lost direction, caught halfway between the old and the new civilizations.

While the Presidio was impressing nobody and the mission was declining, a live-wire English sea captain, William Richardson, founded a more promising settlement — starting with his own tent — near the sheltered Yerba Buena Cove. The cove disappeared long ago as landfills pushed back the sea from hills considered too steep to make settlements on. In fact, the site of Richardson's tent is now high and dry in the middle of Chinatown.

The American era began on 9 July 1846, in the early stages of the Mexican War, when the sloop *U.S.S. Portsmouth* sailed through

Still standing — Mission Dolores recalls San Fran's early days under Spanish colonial rule.

the Golden Gate. Captain John Montgomery led a party ashore and raised the Stars and Stripes flag over the plaza, now called Portsmouth Square after the ship. The ship's cannon then saluted the change of proprietorship. Captain Montgomery himself is immortalized in the name of Montgomery Street in the Financial District.

The peace treaty of Guadalupe Hidalgo was signed on 2 February 1848, only nine days after gold was discovered in California.

Bonanza!

The starter's gun for California's lusty gold rush was fired far from civilization, halfway between Sacramento and Lake Tahoe. At a lumber mill in the Sierra foothills, a carpenter named James Marshall glimpsed the sparkle of the first nugget on 24 January 1848. His boss, the pioneering

City Planners

The layout of San Francisco's streets — grandly logical, on paper — goes back to the early days of Yerba Buena. In 1839 a Swiss settler, Jean-Jacques Vioget, was drafted to draw up a scheme for a town. He based his plan on the Spanish model of a large town square from which streets radiated in a grid.

Under American rule in 1847, an Irish surveyor, Jasper O'Farrell, was given the project of extending the plan. He "invented" Market Street and the much bigger blocks to the south. Both planners were more interested in theory than in practice, which is why the city's long, straight streets go over the tops of hills instead of circling around them. O'Farrell's additional gift to modern motorists is the struggle to find a way to cross Market Street.

tycoon John Augustus Sutter, helped with chemical tests confirming that this was the genuine 23-carat article. Breaking their conspiratorial silence, Sutter soon spread the word.

At first, the reaction in San Francisco was skeptical. Then an ironmonger and huckster, Sam Brannan, appeared in the center of town with a bottle of nuggets, shouting, "Gold! Gold from the American River!" By no coincidence, his sales of shovels and pickaxes picked up instantly. Brannan went on to become the city's first millionaire. Gold, then silver, made San Francisco the capital of the American West.

The city was virtually abandoned overnight as every ambitious, able-bodied citizen rushed to the gold fields. They were followed by the so-called "Forty-Niners," eager prospectors lured from as far away as Australia, China, and Europe. Thousands more boarded ships in New York for the daunting four- to six-month voyage around the tip of South America to San Francisco. On arrival, many a sailor jumped ship at San Francisco and joined the rush for the "Mother of all Lodes."

The population of the shanty-town of San Francisco doubled overnight, then doubled again. In a few months an overgrown hamlet of 2,000 people became a rugged city of 20,000. Before the gold rush fizzled, hundreds of thousands of hopefuls had passed through San Francisco, enriching every entrepreneur from bootmaker to brothel-keeper. It was a wild time, with shortages of everything — housing, food, and law and order — just the climate for fast profits.

Real estate speculators, gamblers, and money-lenders prospered much more handsomely than the miners, especially an immigrant from Germany, one Levi Strauss, who

This statue of firemen, which stands in Russian Hill, marks a vulnerable side of the city, namely its devastation by fire.

unloaded excess fabric in the form of denim trousers that stood up to the hardships of the Sierra: Levi's jeans.

Golden State

California was coining precious metals so fast that the US Congress granted it statehood in 1850, skipping the intermediate dependent status of territory. After the gold ran out, a bonanza of silver, known as the Comstock Lode, followed. Providing the mining equipment and infrastructure for the Virginia City adventure, San Francisco became the fourth-busiest port in the nation, a real town with cultural landmarks like hotels, theaters, and hundreds of saloons and other recreational facilities.

Like many another boom town, San Francisco suffered the side-effects of its prosperity: overcrowding, crime, immorality, and exploitation. It was also a time of disastrous fires, many the work of arsonists. With its haphazardly built shacks and tents, fragile oil lamps, and a tendency for windiness, the town was extremely vulnerable to fire. Crime was also a cause for concern, and the citizens rallied with vigilante groups. If this resulted in the odd lynching, San Franciscans chalked it up to a worthy trend toward an orderly society.

San Francisco drew closer to the rest of the United States in the 1860s with the opening of a direct telegraph line to New York and, at the end of the decade, of the rail link that joined the Atlantic to the Pacific. Four Sacramento merchants, whose names are still affixed to California institutions, joined forces to build the Central Pacific railroad. They were Charles Crocker, Collis P. Huntington, Mark Hopkins,

Chinese on the Railway

The Chinese gold miners who came to California after the 1849 rush were treated coolly, often cruelly, by Americans and Europeans working the Mother Lode. Opportunity beckoned anew during the construction of the transcontinental railway. The Central Pacific found that the Chinese were the best laborers for laying track through hair-raising mountain terrain. Eventually, more than eight out of ten workers on the line were Chinese laborers. Once the project was finished, unemployed Chinese flooded the California job market, prompting more discrimination, both personal and official. Most of the Chinese stopped trying to compete and retreated to the security of their own enclave, San Francisco's Chinatown. Still, there were anti-Chinese riots in 1877.

and Leland Stanford. Their scheme, generously subsidized by the US government, finally came to fruition at Promontory, Utah, in May 1869, when the "golden spike" symbolically spliced eastern and western lines. The "Big Four" entrepreneurs profited a great deal from their monopoly, and the railroad opened the way for unemployed Easterners to descend on the golden West, thus depressing wages, prices, and the economy in general.

Growing Up

In the 1870s and 1880s, San Francisco took on the air of a real city, the key to the West, with a population in the hundreds of thousands and amenities to match. Work on Golden Gate Park, destined to become one of the nation's biggest and best municipal parks, was begun in 1870. City transport took a great leap forward in 1873 when the first cable cars made Nob Hill effortlessly attainable. Next, trolleys brought the more distant areas within reach, and land prices boomed.

The financial prowess of the city was confirmed when a stately United States Mint was built at Fifth and Mission streets. The granite fortress processed a fortune in gold and silver from area mines, producing coins that filled the banks (and pockets) of the West. The Pacific Coast Stock Exchange was founded in 1875, as was a hotel worthy of any tycoon. San Francisco's Palace Hotel, built at a cost of five million dollars, could hold its own with any luxury establishment in the country. Seven stories high, with 800 rooms around an atrium to which guests were conducted in great style, the Palace entertained financiers, statesmen, victorious generals, and other celebrities. Among other elements of modern design, it was meant to be earthquake-proof. Memories of an earthquake during the Civil War period were still resonant.

Falling Down

As San Francisco slept, early on the morning of 18 April 1906, the clocks stopped at 5:12. If there had been a Richter Scale in those days, it would have registered about 8.25. The Great San Francisco Earthquake fissured streets, toppled chimneys, and crumbled thousands of houses, but the worst was yet to come. As gas mains broke, fires erupted — but the water mains also ruptured. The San Francisco Fire Department, whose chief was one of the first victims, could do little to control the flames. The great fire roared out of control for 3 days and wiped out 4 square miles (10 sq. km) of the heart of the city. Crowded aboard ferries heading for Oakland and Marin County, the city's refugees looked back at an apocalyptic skyline under a pall of black smoke.

The Presidio mobilized federal soldiers to control the uncontrollable. They were ordered to dynamite buildings to provide fire breaks, but their knowledge of explosives, and fires, was minimal. During the disaster, the army's miscalculations managed to burn down Chinatown and other tightly packed neighborhoods. Soldiers and National Guardsmen were also assigned to law-and-order duties, resulting in further casualties in the effort to discourage looting. All things considered, the death toll, in the hundreds, could have been worse.

With a quarter of a million San Franciscans homeless, most of them camped out in Golden Gate Park, the pressure to re-build was staggering. Thanks to help from all over the world, reconstruction pushed ahead, and within three years the disaster area had been reclaimed. A clean-up of a different sort brought the downfall of the corrupt regime of Mayor Eugene Schmitz, although His Honor himself managed to avoid jail. Abe Ruef, the power behind city hall, earned himself 14 years at San Quentin prison for extortion.

To demonstrate to the entire world that recovery was complete, the Panama-Pacific International Exposition was held in San Francisco in 1915. It celebrated the opening of the Panama Canal, but more than that the rebirth of a great city. When the tourists had all gone home, the Barbary Coast night life scene — shameless by any standard — was finally tamed under the state legislature's red-light abatement law. With a population of half a million, San Francisco had come a long way from the days of the Wild West.

During the Depression local artists were employed to paint frescoes inside Coit Tower.

Depression and War

During the Great Depression of the 1930s, ambitious public-works projects were designed to provide employment for workers with many skills. The interior of the Coit Tower on Telegraph Hill, dedicated in 1933, was adorned with frescoes by local artists; Franklin Roosevelt's New Deal paid their salaries. The 1930s also put brawnier workers on the payroll, constructing two great bridges: the San Francisco-Oakland Bay Bridge, and the much shorter, but more glamorous, Golden Gate Bridge. The two opened only six months apart. In a mood of growing optimism, yet another San Francisco World's Fair, the Golden

Gate International Exposition, was held on reclaimed land in the bay, subsequently dubbed Treasure Island.

The biggest job-provider of all, World War II, came soon enough. The threat to San Francisco was perceived to be real, and the city staged its first blackout alert only one day after the Japanese attack on Pearl Harbor, in December 1941. The next summer a nervous US government rounded up Japanese residents (including third-generation American citizens) and moved them to the isolation and hardship of internment camps. To try to prove their patriotism, more than 30,000 Japanese-Americans volunteered to fight, and their US Army regiment became the most decorated in the history of American combat.

San Francisco was to play a big part in the war effort as a military and industrial base. As hundreds of Liberty ships rolled from Bay Area assembly lines, 1.6 million American fighting men were funneled through Fort Mason on ships heading for the combat zones. After Japan surrendered in 1945, the U.N. Charter was signed in San Francisco.

Bohemians

San Francisco had always had more than its fair share of non-conformists; the new breeds evolving after the war provoked the world's fascination if not admiration.

First came the Beat Generation, later known disparagingly as "beatniks" (the word was coined after their heyday by the late *Chronicle* columnist Herb Caen). Congregating in North Beach (see page 44), they dressed like revolutionaries, drank coffee while discussing philosophy, read and wrote poetry (some memorable), and supported avant-garde jazz.

In the 1960s the action shifted to the low-rent Haight-Ashbury district (see page 58), where a new species of rebel, less productive intellectually, came to be called "hippies." Ideological powerhouses in San Francisco and Berkeley inspired student radicals all over the United States with their demonstrations for improved civil rights and against American involvement in the Vietnam war.

After the US pulled out of Vietnam, San Francisco's image as a hotbed of radicalism re-focused on a wave of gay rights agitation. In 1978, the first official in the US to proclaim his homosexuality, City Supervisor Harvey Milk, was assassinated, along with Mayor George Moscone. A lenient sentence for the assassin — a disaffected politician — spurred violent protests. The new mayor was a woman — Dianne Feinstein — who would serve 10 years in the post before being elected to the US Senate.

Shaken Again

Earth tremors are a familiar phenomenon in California, but the quake that struck on 17 October 1989 demanded that everyone take notice — in fact, millions of viewers were watching the beginnings of the World Series relayed from San Francisco when the earth shook. Registering 7.1 on the Richter Scale, it was the most severe tremor since 1906, causing billions of dollars' worth of damage and claiming 67 lives. Earthquake-proof modern buildings survived, but many older houses suffered and a large section of the double-decker Bay Bridge collapsed. The elevated two-tier Embarcadero Freeway was damaged as well, and the eyesore was subsequently dismantled after a contentious debate. In a fitting bit of irony, the earthquake can be credited for liberating a long-ignored corner of the city in the decade that followed, paving the way for waterfront development, additional public transportation routes, and a brand new ballpark.

Historical Landmarks

1769 Spanish soldier José Ortega discovers San Francisco Bay while on a scouting mission for Gaspar de Portolá, governor of Spanish California.

1776 On June 29, the first Mass is conducted in San Francisco on the site of Mission Dolores.

1835 William A. Richardson becomes Yerba Buena's first official resident when he erects a shelter in what is now Chinatown.

1846 During the war with Mexico, Captain John B. Montgomery arrives at the site of today's Portsmouth Square and claims Yerba Buena for the United States.

1847 Yerba Buena renamed San Francisco.

1848 James Marshall discovers gold in the Sierra Nevada foothills prompting the great gold rush of 1849.

1873 Andrew Hallidie's cable car takes its inaugural run down Clay Street on August 2.

1906 Two tremors hit San Francisco in the early morning followed by three days of fire. The city is virtually destroyed.

1912 The San Francisco Municipal Railway is created, one of the first publicly owned transit companies in the nation.

1915 The city hosts the Panama-Pacific International Exposition.

1936–1937 The San Francisco-Oakland Bay Bridge opens in 1936, followed in 1937 by the Golden Gate Bridge.

1945 The United Nations charter is signed by representatives from 50 countries in the War Memorial Opera House on 26 June.

1967 Golden Gate Park is the site for the "Human Be-In" and the Haight-Ashbury neighborhood becomes a draw for hippies.

1978 Former city supervisor Dan White assassinates Mayor George Moscone and gay City Supervisor Harvey Milk.

1989 Earthquake causes massive damage throughout Bay Area.

2000 A new Muni route down the Embarcadero to Fisherman's Wharf opens after two years of construction. The San Francisco Giants baseball team plays its first season at Pacific Bell Park in China Basin.

WHERE TO GO

From the social summit of Nob Hill to the ethnic patchwork of the Richmond District, the neighborhoods of San Francisco have their own distinct personalities. If you were lost in the retro Haight-Ashbury district, you'd certainly get the impression it wasn't tidy Noe Valley. Meanwhile, Russian Hill and the Mission District are as different as New York's Upper East Side is from the Lower East Side.

With its well-oiled if oft maligned public transportation system, all of San Francisco is easy to reach. And once you're in the neighborhood you want, it's a great walking town. Walking tours proliferate, targeted at a broad spectrum of interests, from the historical and architectural to the literary or ethnic.

However, before you start off, it's wise to get your bearings with a half-day coach tour. Considering all the hills and the fact that the city is surrounded on three sides by water, its geographical subtleties are not instantly apparent; many a first-time visitor, admiring the steel span of the Bay Bridge, thinks that it's the Golden Gate. Another worthwhile orientation exercise is a one-hour harbor tour, featuring views of the San Francisco skyline.

For the price of an all-day Muni pass you can see a great deal of the city using buses, street cars, and cable cars. Driving around in traffic-heavy San Francisco is not recommended, and locating a parking place is only for the most determined of individuals.

So many hotels, shops, and attractions are centered in Union Square that we begin our survey of San Francisco's sights here. You might want to do the same, as the Visitor Information Center of the San Francisco Convention & Visitors Bureau is right at hand (see page 122), near the

Powell Street cable car terminus in Hallidie Plaza at Market and Powell streets. They can supply you with brochures, maps, and answers to your questions.

DOWNTOWN

Union Square

London has Regent Street, and New York Fifth Avenue. San Francisco does its fashionable shopping around **Union Square**. The names that glitter here stimulate shoppers internationally: Tiffany's, Saks Fifth Avenue, Macy's, Neiman-Marcus, Cartier, and Gucci. In recent years a new crop of stores, including Nike Town and Levis, have joined such hot spots as Virgin Megastore to take the staid edge off Union Square.

Ever surrounded by slow-moving traffic, including a cable-car line, Union Square is a formally landscaped downtown park that sits right on top of the nation's first underground parking structure. The great statue of Victory on top of the Corinthian column in the center of Union Square celebrates Admiral Dewey's 1898 Manila Bay win during the Spanish-American war.

A landmark on the west side of the square, the **Westin St. Francis Hotel,** first opened for business in 1904. Rebuilt, overhauled, ex-

Union Square, where you can shop till you drop or simply stroll the park.

panded, and refurbished over the years (the new lobby alone cost $2 million in 1991), the hotel has welcomed many royals, heads of government, and celebrities. Dozens of hotels, from five-star palaces to modest rooms with shared facilities, are found within a 5-minute walk of Union Square. The area is also populated with many of San Francisco's homeless, who make their quiet appeal to the consciences of the city's well-heeled passers-by.

Have yourself an adventure in Chinatown, 24 blocks wide and a world away.

On the east side of the square, **Maiden Lane** runs into Stockton Street. The prim name is an affectation. Maiden Lane was once known as Morton Street, under which alias it was a hotbed of Barbary Coast vice. The post-earthquake fire of 1906 extinguished the red lights, and nowadays it's a pleasant and well-appointed pedestrian street of designer shops.

The building at 140 Maiden Lane is the only San Francisco work by the architect Frank Lloyd Wright. The ramp is reminiscent of Wright's revolutionary Guggenheim Museum in New York.

☞ Chinatown

Immerse yourself totally in the experience and lose yourself in the 24-square-block confines of San Francisco's Chinatown. Here the second biggest Chinese community outside Asia (New York's is first) crowds into the exotic emporia, temples, tea houses, and restaurants that are so good the residents of Canton would be jealous. By way of infrastructure there are Chinese banks, schools, law offices, travel agencies, video shops, bookstores, laundries, and factories recalling the sweatshops of earlier times.

Since gold rush days, most of the Chinese in San Francisco, and the United States in general, have had their roots in Guangdong (Kwangtung) province, whose capital is Canton. Thus the Cantonese dialect and cuisine are often encountered here. But newer immigrants from other Chinese provinces, and from Indochina, Hong Kong, and Taiwan, have added their own distinctive flavor to the melting pot.

In order to enter Chinatown through the front door, approach it from the Union Square area or the Financial District. The **Chinatown Gate,** at Grant Avenue and Bush Street, has the classic design of a Chinese village gate, but it

---

Waiting for the Big One

San Francisco sits right on top of the San Andreas Fault, a major fracture in the earth's crust that runs northwest from the Gulf of California for 600 miles (965 km), passing beneath the city and separating Point Reyes from the mainland. The BART subway tunnel between San Francisco and Oakland was bored right through the fault.

The Baja California peninsula and the coast to the west of the fault are moving north relative to the rest of North America, at an average of half an inch (1 cm) per year. There has been no movement along the San Francisco section of the fault since the disastrous earthquake of 1906, but experts predict that there's a 50/50 chance of another major quake — the dreaded Big One — occurring within the next 30 years.

dates from 1970. Bulging with souvenir shops and restaurants, always bustling Grant Avenue is the prime tourist promenade of Chinatown. But be sure to veer off to find a more authentic experience on Broadway and Stockton Street.

Two blocks ahead, across the California Street cable car tracks, **Old St. Mary's Church** was San Francisco's Roman Catholic cathedral during most of the second half of the 19th century. Now it is a parish church. Under the clock is an inscription, "Son Observe the Time and Fly from Evil." That's "son," not "sun" — it was aimed at prospective patrons of the brothels that used to operate across the street.

Portsmouth Square, where slow-motion *tai chi* exercises are performed and where old men play checkers, happens to be very important historically. This was the main plaza of the original Mexican colony that became San Francisco. The square sits atop a parking garage and features a children's playground, benches, and a perfect view of the Transamerica Pyramid in the Financial District.

The **Bank of Canton** at 743 Washington Street preserves the delightful **Old Chinese Telephone Exchange** in the original, spectacularly Chinese setting of red pillars and soaring tile roofs. This was the headquarters of the Chinatown telephone exchange, where operators could deal with subscribers in English as well as in Chinese dialects. After World War II the arrival of dial telephones put these talented linguists out of work.

The back streets of San Francisco's Chinatown meet almost all specifications for those in search of the mysteries of the Far East. Typically, **Ross Alley,** up Washington Street from Grant Avenue, is both exotic and, since the 1980s, nicely paved. The little shops and factories are just what you'd expect to find in an alley beyond the tourist zone of Kowloon — garment factories, jewelry shops, sellers of miniature

Formerly known as the Old Chinese Telephone Exchange, this delightful building is now home to the Bank of Canton.

Buddhist shrines, and a one-chair barber shop. Here, too, is the Golden Gate Fortune Cookie Company, from where those typically American-Chinese pastries originate. Watch the deft hands of the operators folding moist cookies around slips of paper enigmatically foretelling the fate of future customers at Chinese restaurants around the world. You can purchase bags of fresh almond or fortune cookies from the ladies in the factory.

Although Grant Avenue constantly teems with tourists, **Stockton Street** is busier still; it's where the Chinese community shop for food and essentials. Soak up the sights, sounds, and smells of Chinese supermarkets, open-air vegetable markets, fish markets, herbalists, delicatessens, pastry shops, and tea rooms. On the roof of the modern Chinatown branch of the US Post Office at Stockton and Clay streets is a Chinese temple — the **Kong Chow Temple** — with a historic altar and a view of the bay from its balcony. At 843 Stockton Street, the headquarters of the **Chinese Six Companies** (officially the Chinese Consolidated Benevolent Association) is a garishly decorated building dating from the early 20th century. The organization was central to the fight against anti-Chinese discrimination, which persisted until relatively recent times.

Financial District and Jackson Square

Heading northeast into the Financial District, stop in the **Crocker Galleria,** an airy, glass-domed shopping mall on three floors. It was inspired by Milan's Galleria Vittorio Emanuelle, built more than a century earlier. Across Sutter Street from the mall, don't miss the **Hallidie Building,** named after the man who put the cable car on track. Dating from 1917, it might have been the first "glass curtain wall" building anywhere; the glass-and-metal façade hangs from the top instead of helping to support the structure. Apart from the boldness of the engineering, there are wonderful frills, such as the disguised external fire escapes. The ground floor of the Hallidie Building is now shared by a bank and a post office. Office workers take their lunch breaks on **Belden Alley,** off Bush Street between Pine and Kearney streets. Here, a half dozen delicious restaurants offer outdoor dining Monday through Saturday until 10pm.

Place names in San Francisco tend to be straightforward, but just as North Beach is not a beach, **Jackson Square** is not a square. The name refers to a block of buildings bounded by Jackson, Montgomery, Gold, and Sansome streets, just north of the Transamerica Pyramid. The city's pioneers crudely reclaimed this area from the bay with ballast from arriving ships, and in many cases the ships themselves, abandoned by crewmen who joined the gold rush. This was destined to become one of the most infamous areas of the Barbary Coast. A relatively small collection of low-rise, thick-walled brick offices, banks, shops, and factories miraculously withstood the quake and subsequent fires in 1906. In the middle of the 20th century, when the district's historic and architectural importance was discovered, restoration of the landmarks began. Today, Jackson Square has become the elegant place to have a law office, ad agency, art gallery, or antiques shop.

BESIDE THE BAY

San Francisco's big, beautiful waterfront has undergone a facelift. It began when the 1989 earthquake doomed the elevated Embarcadero Freeway, an eyesore that cost nearly half as much to dismantle as it had to build. With the demise of the "abominable autobahn," as the San Francisco *Chronicle* called it at the outset, unobstructed views of the Ferry Building and harbor were revealed, and lo-cal developers and planners took a long, hard look around. By now, the construction crews have gone home (one hopes), leaving a length of new Muni tracks and inviting plazas on which to linger while you admire the imported palm trees that

Fresh produce and a fresh ocean breeze quayside, at The Embarcadero.

Spanning San Francisco and Oakland, the lovely Bay Bridge is often mistaken for the Golden Gate by visitors.

decorate the boulevard. Called **The Embarcadero** (Spanish for "quay"), this piece of the bay stretches from the new baseball stadium at King Street all the way to Fisherman's Wharf.

Rumbling almost overhead near Harrison Street you'll get a dramatic view of the **San Francisco-Oakland Bay Bridge.** The bridge, anchored in the middle on Yerba Buena Island, is 8 miles (13 km) long. Like the more celebrated Golden Gate Bridge, it was built during the Depression days of the 1930s. Unlike the Golden Gate, the Bay Bridge wears a necklace of lights to add to the romance of San Francisco's nights.

Just northwest of the bridge's take-off for Oakland is the **Ferry Building,** where you may board a Golden Gate commuter ferry to Sausalito. The station and its multi-stage tower date from the turn of the 20th century. The Embarcadero is a very mixed bag between the Ferry Building and Fisherman's Wharf. Walkers, joggers, bicyclists, and skate boarders make the most of its wide sidewalks. The maritime activities that made this a great port, such as whaling and countless, varied ferries, have either disappeared or moved to the railhead at Oakland across the bay. What's left are the occasional luxury liner welcoming passengers bound for Alaska, harbor cruise ships, sightseeing boats, and deep-sea fishing charters.

Fisherman's Wharf

California's most visited attraction is Disneyland, which can be an expensive family outing; in second place is San Francisco's **Fisherman's Wharf,** which is free, sort of. The area of amusements, souvenir shops, bongo drummers, peripatetic mimes, and generally unstoppable street life runs along Jefferson Street from around Pier 43 to beyond Pier 47.

Pier 39, a tourist complex constructed of recycled lumber from old wharves, is the major draw: It now claims more than 13 million visitors a year. They come to shop, snack or dine, watch street performers, ride a double-deck carousel, admire the view of the bay, take a tour, rent a yacht, or dis-

---

Persistent Pinnipeds

The bewhiskered sea lions have been barking at Pier 39 since 1990, evidently attracted by a herring bonanza and a totally safe, comfortable haven. Although the big fellows put a potentially profitable yacht-parking zone out of action, nobody could convince them to leave, and federal law forbids harassing them. Pier 39 discovered that the smelly squatters were good for business; a sculpture was commissioned as a tribute to the blubbery marine mammals, and for tourists who want to know more about their swimming, feeding, and breeding habits, there are explanatory tours.

cover what all that barking is about. No, that's not a pack of eager hounds on K-Dock, but up to 600 sea lions preening themselves and arguing over the best spot to sunbathe.

At the heart of it all is a concentration of fish restaurants. Exacting local gourmets may look down on them, citing that their prices are quite high for preparations that are quite pedestrian. Nevertheless, they're handy places for fresh local and imported seafood with a view. The "fast food" offered by outdoor stalls here — shrimp and crab cocktails, and clam chowder in an edible pot — is popular, but if crab isn't in season (November through May), those crustaceans you're eating have been frozen. The truth is, the fishing fleet that you can survey here (the oldest boats are more prominently placed) contributes only a small percentage of the catch needed to feed all of San Francisco.

At Pier 45, a boat of a different sort is worth a look. ***U.S.S. Pampanito,*** a World War II submarine credited with the sinking of six Japanese ships, is open to visitors (admission is charged). Even though the sub is not submerged, some landlubbers feel a touch of claustrophobia in the narrow passages and dimly lit operations center.

Inland from Fisherman's Wharf, the **Cannery** occupies a vast red-brick building from the early 20th century. It

Sea lions have taken up residence — and stolen the show — at Pier 39.

was an important fruit-packing plant, cleverly converted into an attractive browsing, eating, and entertainment area, including a small museum of local history.

Ghirardelli Square is a bigger shopping and eating zone in a red-brick complex that began as a chocolate factory. A stylish alternative to the knick-knack-and-T-shirt boutiques of Jefferson Street, the enterprises here sell toys, jewelry, fashionable clothes, and even museum-worthy folk art from several continents, as well as chocolate — although the well-regarded local brand is now manufactured in a high-tech plant across the bay.

Victorian Park, overlooking the Aquatic Park Marina and the bay, is a pleasant place to break from the heavy footwork of sightseeing and shopping. Flocks of tourists spend more time than they had planned in this park, queuing up for the cable car. This is where the Powell-Hyde line is pushed onto the turntable before heading back toward Union Square.

Farther along the beach, the **National Maritime Museum** is grandly titled, but is more remarkable for its

Highway Robbery

Since its foundation in the middle of the 19th century, San Quentin has "entertained" many thousands of convicts, but few as colorful as C.E. Boles, alias "Black Bart." From 1875 to 1883 he specialized in holding up Wells Fargo stagecoaches — always politely, without firing a shot. Among the other ways he annoyed and embarrassed the law was to leave little poems at the scene of the crime, poems so bad that even Black Bart wrote, "And if for any cause I'm hung/Let it be for my verses." Traced by the laundry mark on a handkerchief he dropped, the gentlemanly desperado drew seven years at San Quentin. He was out in four: good behavior, of course.

building than for the exhibits, which are mostly model ships and photographs. It was built in 1939 in a streamlined design resembling a beached passenger ship, and there are appropriate nautical murals.

Real historic ships, rocking gently against the pier, are near at hand at **Hyde Street Pier.** More than a century old, the sidewheel ferry *Eureka* was the world's largest passenger-and-car ferry in its day. Vintage cars are parked aboard, as they were when the ferries constituted a link in US Highway 101. Other old ships that you can board include the *C.A. Thayer,* a three-masted lumber-carrying schooner, as well as *Balclutha,* a square-rigger launched in Scotland in 1886. Hyde Street Pier is so educational that even the toilets contain tableaux explaining the evolution of "heads" on ships, from the days when sailors had to "go" overboard.

One more historic ship on display, the Liberty Ship *S.S. Jeremiah O'Brien,* a veteran of the famous D-Day invasion of France, is moored at Pier 3, a memorial to the World War II personnel of the US Merchant Marine. More than 2,700 ships like it were produced between 1941 and 1945.

Escape from Alcatraz

Officially, nobody ever escaped from Alcatraz. In all, 39 prisoners attempted it: 27 were caught, 7 were killed, and 5 have never been found but are assumed drowned.

In 1962, at the very end of the island's grim history, John Paul Scott made it to the San Francisco shore by greasing his body to help withstand the cold. A party of students found him clinging to the rocks at Fort Point, just below the Golden Gate Bridge, completely exhausted. Not knowing he was an escaped prisoner, they helpfully called the police to rescue the poor fellow in his hour of need.

The piers here are part of **Fort Mason,** which was head-quarters of the San Francisco Port of Embarkation during the Second World War. Over 1.5 million troops and 20 million tons of cargo passed through here on their way to combat zones. After the war, operations shifted to Oakland, and now the fort is part of the Golden Gate National Recreational Area.

At sea level, a complex of nine buildings is now devoted to entertainment, recreation, education, as well as other cultural initiatives. Four museums operate in the Fort Mason Center: the Afro-American Historical and Cultural Society, the Italian Educational Cultural Center, the Mexican Museum (which will be moving near Yerba Buena Gardens in 2001), and the San Francisco Craft and Folk Art Museum. The exhibitions change several times a year.

Just a stone's throw from the city, Alcatraz saw many a prisoner attempt escape to San Francisco's seductive shores.

Alcatraz

All harbor excursions offer a close look at the moody former prison isle called **Alcatraz,** but the only way to step ashore and tour the abandoned cell-blocks is via the Blue and Gold Fleet from Pier 41. In summer and at weekends the tours are soon sold out; you have to book early, sometimes weeks ahead.

The vital difference between Alcatraz and its French equivalent, Devil's Island, is that Alcatraz looks out on a seductive city, not a hostile jungle; with the wind in the right direction, the prisoners could even hear the sounds of civilization just beyond their reach.

Alcatraz (from the Spanish *Isla de los Alcatraces*, or Pelican Island) served as America's most forbidding federal penitentiary from 1934 to 1963. It's said that Attorney General Robert Kennedy closed down the dilapidated prison when he discovered that it would have been cheaper (and certainly more comfortable) to keep the inmates at the Waldorf Astoria Hotel. Now the island is operated by the US National Park Service. A self-guided trail has been laid out, covering the principal areas of interest, or you can join in a more specialized walking tour led by a park ranger. Inside the cell-block, you can rent an audio tape (available in English, French, German, Italian, Japanese, and Spanish), on which tour directions are interspersed with a documentary based on the pertinent testimony of retired wardens and ex-prisoners. You'll see the cells of Al Capone and "the Birdman," Robert Stroud; roam the central corridor, ironically known as Broadway; have a chance to step inside a punishment cell; and check a typical menu in the dining hall. Alcatraz food is said to have been the best in the federal prison system — designed to give the inmates one less reason to riot.

By one count, 39 prisoners tried and failed to escape from the island. Two made it to the mainland, only to be picked up almost immediately, and five are listed as missing, officially presumed drowned — but did they? Here the imagination takes over.

Marina District

The earthquake of 1989 put the Marina on the world's television screens: Because the district is built on land reclaimed from the bay, dozens of houses succumbed to the 7.1 shock. The land was created from dredged sand after the 1906 quake to provide a site for the Panama-Pacific International Exposition of 1915.

Other than the earthquake problem, the Marina is a desirable place to live or visit, with its charming pastel-painted houses and varied up-market shopping on Chestnut Street. **Marina Green** is a fashionable bayside park for sunbathing, jogging, skating, biking, and kite flying.

An eye-catching monument from the 1915 World's Fair, the splendid pink **Palace of Fine Arts,** restored and reinforced, survived the tremor of 1989. This was a lucky development, for both its dreamy contribution to local

Pretty in pink — the Palace of Fine Arts dates from the 1915 World's Fair.

The tree-lined Presidio — the loveliest ex-military establishment you'll ever see.

pseudo-classical architecture, as well as its utility. The palace is now the site of the **Exploratorium,** also known as the Museum of Science, Art and Human Perception. Even an inquisitive octopus would not get his fill of "hands-on" exhibits at this endlessly instructive and entertaining center. Children become animated and intent, and parents and grandparents insist on their turn. Founded by Dr. Frank Oppenheimer (brother of the atomic Robert), the institution amounts to a big workshop.

The Presidio

Hundreds of thousands of invigorating cypress, eucalyptus, and pine trees shade the 1,480 acres (600 hectares) of the **Presidio** of San Francisco, the prettiest ex-military establishment you're ever likely to see. Founded as a Spanish fort in 1776, then active on the American side in several wars, it was belatedly converted to civilian life during the 1990s as part of the Golden Gate National Recreation Area. The beauty of the landscape dates from the late 19th century, when the trees were planted on what had been forbidding, rocky heights.

Feel free to explore the Presidio, either by bus or car or on foot, for its tastefully designed and impeccably maintained headquarters buildings, officers' quarters, and even model enlisted men's barracks.

The Presidio **museum,** at Lincoln Boulevard and Funston Avenue, is full of San Francisco military and civilian history. Once a hospital, it was built in 1864. A spacious military **cemetery** tells of battles going back to the Indian Wars. Not far away is an army pet cemetery, rich in anecdotal dog and cat gravestones.

Hiding under the southern end of the Golden Gate Bridge, mid-19th-century **Fort Point** is an ominous looking relic with a heart-stopping view of the strait. The National Park Service now runs tours through what was once the US Army's only brick fortress defending the West Coast against naval attack. The threat was considered real at the time of the Civil War, when it was suspected that the Confederate Navy might show up. As in so many military designs, this coastal artillery installation became out of date technologically as soon as it was built. Engineering enthusiasts will appreciate the almost-close-enough-to-touch view of the underside of the great bridge.

Golden Gate

Perhaps the bridge is thrilling because the pylons, as tall as 65-story buildings, taper upward like the spires of an Art

---

The Bridge: the Score

When it was built, the Golden Gate Bridge was the world's longest and tallest suspension structure. Here are some statistics:

Total length (including the approaches): 8,981 ft (2,737 m).

Height of towers: 746 ft (227 m).

Total weight on San Francisco pier foundation: 363,000 tons (329,000 metric tons).

Total length of wire in cables: 80,000 miles (129,000 km).

Traffic per year: 30 million vehicles.

Fare: $3 arriving in San Francisco; leaving town it's free.

Deco cathedral. It's not just the grace of its arches, though; you have to see the fog devouring its towers while the sun flashes on the water below, where sailboards zigzag in and out of the wake of ferryboats. Whatever the magic, one of America's favorite bridges is a wonder of engineering. In the little park at the southern end a statue honors the designer, Joseph B. Strauss of Chicago, also responsible for the Arlington Memorial Bridge in Washington DC.

Here you can see and touch a sample cross-section of one of the cables supporting the bridge — composed of 27,572 wires for a diameter of 3 feet (0.9 meters).

Chief Engineer Strauss began promoting the idea of a bridge in 1917. Many opponents of the project feared a bridge would deface the dramatic strait; others simply felt it couldn't be done, as tidal currents sometimes reach 60 mph (100 km/h). After "two decades and 200 million words," as Strauss put it, the people believed him. Construction began in 1933. Eleven construction workers died, but 19 others were saved by the safety net Strauss designed. The bridge opened for traffic in May 1937.

A bridgeworker's job is never done, of course, so a crew of more than 40 is occupied year-round to clean and paint, using some 5,000 gallons (22,730 liters) of

Strolling across the Golden Gate is not for the faint of heart — you can feel it sway.

paint per year. The color, called "international orange," is the most easily visible in fog, and has won prizes for resisting salt, rain, sun, and wind.

Charles de Gaulle walked across the bridge in 1960. So can you, in either direction. It's about a 2-mile (3-km) trip — an invigorating, windy outing for the whole family. But leave behind anyone with a fear of heights; it's about 220 ft (67 m) straight down to the water, and you can feel the bridge swaying.

THE HILLS

The hills of San Francisco provide uplifting views of the city and the bay — just the thing for millionaires in search of a homestead or tourists merely wanting to borrow a panorama. Of the 40 or so hills available, we've chosen a few of the most appealing, with some detours into the valleys.

Telegraph Hill is named after the primitive semaphore set up here in gold rush days to relay news of ship arrivals to traders down in the Financial District. In 1876 a group of benefactors bought the top of the hill and gave it to the city for a park. Students of architecture and landscaping will be delighted to see how it turned out; the houses and gardens clinging to the hillsides are charmingly original. For a good look, walk the **Filbert Street steps** down to Sansome Street.

Sprouting from Telegraph Hill is landmark **Coit Tower,** a reinforced-concrete column of no practical value but considerable grace. Notwithstanding the version often recounted by tourist guides, it was not designed to resemble a fire-hose nozzle. It was merely an artful way of fulfilling the bequest of Lillie Hitchcock Coit, an unconventional 19th-century woman with close ties to the fire brigade, to build a beautiful monument. You have to pay to ride to the top for one of the best vantage points in town, but there is no charge to view the fine murals, which depict California life during the Great Depression years in Socialist Realist style, in the lobby.

North Beach

A landlocked valley between Telegraph Hill and Russian Hill, **North Beach** is not a beach at all. Although Chinatown is making inroads, this is the heart of the Italian community, where Columbus Day is a very big deal. North Beach is the place to find real Italian *prosciutto, gelato,* and *cappuccino*. It was once also the focus of the city's artistic and intellectual life, where poets and Bohemians attempted to influence the culture.

The center of the neighborhood is **Washington Square,** a small park with a bust of Benjamin Franklin in the middle. People from Chinatown arrive in the morning to do their martial arts exercises. The changing complexion of the area is also reflected in the **Church of Saints Peter and Paul,** where one of the morning masses is said in Chinese every Sunday.

North Beach's main street, Columbus Avenue, has several claims to fame. Lawrence Ferlinghetti's **City Lights Bookstore** was the headquarters of what became known as the Beat Generation, and earnest intellectuals still take seats there and browse.

Other thinkers and escapists stake out the nearby cafés, rich in Italian aromas and heady atmosphere. One further cultural note: A **plaque** set on the wall of the Condor nightspot at Broadway and Columbus claims that this is the birthplace of both topless (in 1964) and bottomless (1969) entertainment.

Russian Hill

You're unlikely to find any Russians on genteel Russian Hill, or not alive anyway. In the earliest days of San Francisco this was a burial ground for the crews of Russian trapping and fishing ships.

Bound by Francisco, Hyde, Lombard, and Taylor streets, Russian Hill is best reached by public transport, owing to driving and parking problems. Some of the streets here are so steep they simply turn into stairways. As for streets that are fit for cars — with very brave or foolhardy drivers at their wheel — have a look at Filbert Street, which is between Leavenworth and Hyde streets. The grade here is 31.5 percent, the steepest in the city, according to the municipal Bureau of Engineering. If you insist on driving it, be sure your brakes are in top-notch condition and take the crest *very* slowly.

The "crookedest street in the world," Lombard Street is one of the prettiest, too.

Another amazing thoroughfare is the 1000 block of Lombard Street, the **"crookedest street in the world,"** between Hyde and Leavenworth. To ease the stress, eight switchbacks were installed, cutting the incline to a mere 18 percent.

Among architectural highlights, see the **Octagonal house** at 1067 Green Street, which was built before the Civil War. At the time there was a theory that eight-sided houses were better for the health than the usual quadrangular design. The only other house of this kind here, 2645 Gough Street, is open three afternoons per month. Check with the Colonial Dames of America, Tel. (415) 441-7512.

Cable Cars

A genuine National Landmark on the go! If you thought cable cars were just a tourist gimmick, don't mention it to the San Franciscans aboard. It's quite clearly one of the most enjoyable and exciting ways to travel, and one which you simply must experience.

Whether crammed into the passenger compartment, braving the elements on benches facing outwards, or even standing on the running board and hanging on, you could never have known that 9.5 mph (15 km/h) would feel so reckless. The crewmen are gregarious, and chat and joke with the passengers, but they are very stern about where you sit or stand; follow their orders.

Way to go! Hangers-on travel San Francisco-style — by cable car, that is.

The cable cars themselves are powerless. To travel, the gripman has to clamp onto the moving cable, which propels the car until he releases the grip and signals the brakeman to apply the brakes. The grip mechanism and the brakes have to be replaced quite often, and when a cable breaks everything must stop until it can be mended.

San Francisco Highlights

Two or three days is barely long enough to see the city, but if you're tight for time, here are the most popular places to spend those precious hours.

Alcatraz Island: A little bleak for young kids, but fascinating if you have an interest in prisons. The view of the city is an added bonus (see page 38).

Cable Cars: A bit of history on wheels and immensely fun. Go early to avoid the lines on Powell Street or try catching a car a few stops above the turn-around (see page 46).

Chinatown: A walk along crowded Stockton Street on an afternoon or weekend is literally sensational — among the outdoor vegetable markets, the smell of fish, the old women pushing past with their full shopping baskets, and the incessant traffic, you'll be awash in sights, smells, and sounds (see page 26).

Fisherman's Wharf: 13 million tourists can't all be wrong, can they? Purely and simply a tourist attraction, and a fine place to pick up a sweatshirt (see page 33).

Golden Gate Bridge: If you don't have the time or energy to walk across the bridge, make your way to the little park underneath (see page 41).

Golden Gate Park: One of the loveliest open urban spaces in the country, providing nature walks and cultural opportunities (see page 58).

Union Square: Convenient, high-ticket shopping and excellent dining in one central location.

Yerba Buena Gardens: An example of urban renewal in all its glory, including cultural pursuits, excellent family entertainment, as well as rampant consumerism (see page 51).

Outrageously out of date, the cable car system has often been threatened with closure for efficiency reasons, but in 1964 the cable cars were added to the National Register of Historic Places. In the 1980s all the lines were shut down for nearly two years for top-to-bottom renovation. The ancient cars, back in action, are too close to San Francisco's heart to be endangered again for a long time.

Nob Hill

The "nob" in Nob Hill is short for "nabob," an old-fashioned English word from India for a rich and powerful man. The nabobs who settled on this smart California Street hilltop had made their fortune in the gold rush days, as often as not in the railroad business. All four rail barons — Charles Crocker, Mark Hopkins, Leland Stanford, and Collis Huntington — built private palaces here in the 1870s, as the newfangled cable car was then making the hill accessible. Three of them now have their names attached to luxury hotels on Nob Hill, the exception being Charles Crocker, whose family very generously gave their land as the site of Grace Cathedral (see page 49).

Today, five-star hotels and elite apartment blocks have displaced all the old mansions, except one. Behind its brass filigreed fence, the **Pacific Union Club** at 1000 California Street was once the 42-room home of one James Flood, a saloon-keeper who became one of the kings of the Comstock Silver Lode. Although the interior of the mansion was entirely burned out in the 1906 fire, the brownstone sobriety remains intact. This traditional gentlemen's club, also known as the P-U, is the city's most exclusive. Unlike the club, the fashionable hotels of Nob Hill admit women. In fact, just about anyone can slip into the hotel lobbies or have a drink in any of the attractive bars.

Grace Cathedral, an Episcopal tribute to Gothic style, was built in 1964. Although it does resemble Notre Dame of Paris, this impressive church is built of concrete and steel — not stone — as an anti-earthquake precaution. The gilded bronze doors of the east entrance are replicas of the 15th-century *Gates of Paradise* sculpted by Lorenzo Ghiberti for the Baptistery in Florence.

MARKET STREET

Mostly as straight as an arrow, the wide diagonal of Market Street marches from the bay-front right to the edge of Twin Peaks. It starts promisingly among ambi-

In Huntington Park, an elegant fountain exemplifies the tone of affluent Nob Hill.

tious skyscrapers, then rambles on to the sort of neighborhood you wouldn't want to linger in.

Nearest to the Embarcadero is the **Rincon Center,** a modern development of shops, offices, and apartments attached to what was originally a branch post office. The federal government sponsored the murals, depicting events from the history of San Francisco. A splendid atrium has a free-falling waterfall decorating its center.

Of all the imposing buildings along Market Street, two hotels stand out for their originality, although they couldn't be more dissimilar. The **Sheraton Palace Hotel,** at Market and New Montgomery streets, was the city's original luxury hotel, expensively redone at the end of the 1980s. Its awesome, glass-domed Garden Court is a sumptuous setting for breakfast, tea, dinner, or just a peek at how the other half lives. The contemporary **San Francisco Marriott Hotel,** at Market and Fourth, contrasts with its very daring post-modern design. Some critics think it looks like a 40-story jukebox. Love it or hate it, it's impossible to miss.

A shopping mall with a distinctive flavor is the **San Francisco Centre** (note the UK spelling, which is supposed to add to the up-market feeling). It has raised the tone at Fifth and Market streets with its incredible spiral escalators, still a source of amazement for many visitors. The top five floors all belong to the Nordstrom department store.

South of Market

For some years now, South of Market Street, or **SoMa,** has been in upheaval, as gentrification razes buildings and raises rents in what had long been the dreariest of underprivileged neighborhoods — now quickly becoming the city's hippest enclave and the center of Internet activity. The biggest

SoMa's got the MOMA — and the Yerba Buena Gardens, too!

of the projects that has revolutionized the area is **Yerba Buena Gardens,** which includes the **Moscone Convention Center,** named after the assassinated Mayor George Moscone (see page 22). It is an enormous exhibition complex, mostly underground, and big enough to hold a political convention (the Democrats staged theirs here in 1984). The lovely gardens have brought a welcome presence to the area along with enough amusements to keep visitors busy for an entire day. For youngsters, there's a carousel that originally graced the long demolished Playland at the Beach, an ice skating rink, bowling alley, and **Zeum,** a hands-on technology/arts center specifically geared to older kids and teenagers. Across Howard Street you'll no doubt be drawn toward the new **Sony Metreon,** a huge entertainment complex with 15 theaters (including an Imax), a half dozen restaurants, cutting edge technology stores, and an interactive video room, the "Airtight Garage." The games actually appeal to grownups as well as kids, unless you're sensitive to noise, of which there's a great deal.

The most prominent building nearby is the stunning **San Francisco Museum of Modern Art** (MOMA), whose works include paintings and sculptures by Matisse, Klee, Pollock, and other major artists of the modernist schools; included, too, is an extensive collection of photography. In the daytime, art lovers come here to inspect the galleries, shop in the gift store, and lunch in the café. SoMa also supports a lively nightlife venue along Folsom Street.

Tucked inside a rather nondescript building a half-block from the Metreon is the **Cartoon Art Museum** (814 Mission Street). Endowed by *Peanuts* creator Charles M. Schulz, the museum is a treasure trove of artwork and books, featuring underground and mainstream cartoonists from America and abroad. Closed Mondays, the museum charges a modest entry fee.

THE NEIGHBORHOODS

Mission District

Mission Street runs parallel to Market Street until Van Ness Avenue, where it bends into a north–south direction and becomes the main stem of the Mission District. It is an ethnically diverse area, the neighborhood of choice for Central and South Americans, and San Franciscans seeking somewhat affordable housing.

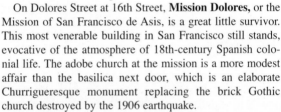 On Dolores Street at 16th Street, **Mission Dolores,** or the Mission of San Francisco de Asis, is a great little survivor. This most venerable building in San Francisco still stands, evocative of the atmosphere of 18th-century Spanish colonial life. The adobe church at the mission is a more modest affair than the basilica next door, which is an elaborate Churrigueresque monument replacing the brick Gothic church destroyed by the 1906 earthquake.

The restored ceiling of the elongated, narrow church of Mission Dolores is decorated with brightly colored Indian motifs; the carved altars came from Mexico. A small museum on the premises shows how the California missions were constructed, and there is a collection of photographs of a visit here by the Pope in the 1980s. A walled-in cemetery beside the church also serves as a botanical garden, a restful place with more than 100 varieties of flowers, most of them in bloom. A statue of the founder of the mission system, Father Junípero Serra, was the work of blind sculptor Arthur Putnam.

The merchants along **24th Street** below Dolores Street call their thoroughfare the Mission District's "Boulevard of the Americas," and a Mexican national holiday is celebrated here on 5 May (see page 94) with a colorful parade. There are dozens of brilliantly tinted Mexican-style murals, as well as plenty of exotic grocery stores and several restaurants offering tempting Central and South American cuisine. Above Dolores Street on 24th Street is the central artery of **Noe Valley,** a neighborhood of Victorian houses, dogs, and plenty of babies in strollers and backpacks.

Civic Center

Monumental grandeur is the keynote of the San Francisco Civic Center, built after the 1906 quake with unbounded optimism and funds. The scope and size of this center of municipal government can't be matched anywhere else in the United States.

San Francisco's formidable City Hall is especially poignant when lit up at night.

City Hall rather resembles the Capitol building in Washington, but the black and gold dome of the San Francisco structure (patterned on St. Peter's in Rome) is even higher. Inside the great rotunda, over the clock, is inscribed the name of James Rolph, Jr. ("Mayor 1912–1931"). Surely any first-class dictator would envy "Sunny Jim" Rolph this monument; the ceremonial staircase all but cries out for magnificent evening gowns and tails.

The **Main Public Library** occupies a new, faux-Beaux-Arts building across from its old genuine Beaux-Arts headquarters, which will reopen as the Asian Art Museum (now in Golden Gate Park) in the year 2001. **United Nations Plaza,** named after the world organization founded in San Francisco in 1945, is the scene of a farmers' market on Wednesday and Sunday. Otherwise it's a haunt for the homeless.

On Van Ness Avenue, behind City Hall, an ensemble of nicely balanced buildings includes the **Opera House, Symphony Hall,** and the **California State Office Building.**

The Castro

This is a friendly neighborhood, well stocked with coffee shops, boutiques, and bookshops, but you'll soon notice something is different. Castro Street is the main street of the

A streetcar takes its route through the Castro district, cultural heart of San Francisco's gay community.

district most closely associated with San Francisco's gay community — which constitutes a numerically and politically significant proportion of the city's population. The biggest annual parade in San Francisco is the Lesbian/Gay Pride Celebration in June, which involves the participation of hundreds of thousands of people of many orientations.

When the Muni Metro train stops at Castro Street station, you surface in **Harvey Milk Plaza,** which is named after the first avowedly gay member of the city board of supervisors. He was martyred in the City Hall assassination of 1977.

The wittily named specialized shops of Castro Street are the most unusual monuments, except for the classic 1920s cinema palace, the **Castro Theatre**, in Art Deco style. At 2362A Market Street, the **Names Project** is the workshop in which an enormous quilt continues to grow, commemorating victims of AIDS.

Up the hill from here, **Twin Peaks** are not quite the tallest hills in town, but nearly. The lucky folk whose houses are perched on the hillsides enjoy unparalleled views of the San Francisco skyline and the bay.

Japantown

A modern interpretation of a five-tiered round pagoda towers above Japantown, or Nihonmachi (between Geary, Webster, California and Octavia streets), where the city's sizeable Japanese population comes to stock up on ethnic food, books, and films. The **Peace Pagoda**, a gift from the people of Japan, is surmounted by a graceful nine-ringed spire symbolizing the highest virtue and supporting a golden sphere with a flaming head.

Japanese people have lived in San Francisco since the 1860s. The darkest era was World War II, when Japanese-Americans

The Peace Pagoda — a gift from Japan — towers high above Japantown.

were sent to internment camps (see page 21). After the war, many returned, however, and during the 1960s the Japan Center transformed the area into a commercial zone with air-conditioned shopping malls, offices, sushi bars, restaurants, and a hotel and spa. Bibliophiles will enjoy browsing in the Kinokuniya bookstore, an enormous book-shop specializing in books and magazines about Japan.

Just east of Japantown, at Gough and Geary streets, **St. Mary's Cathedral** is the city's most unusual religious structure, replacing a smaller Catholic cathedral destroyed by fire in 1962. Its modern architecture zooms heaven-ward. American and Italian architects and engineers joined forces in geometric experiments — the cupola is described as a hyperbolic parabola, with a volume of nearly 2,135,000 cubic ft (60,000 cubic m). The ingredients combine in a harmonious whole, with red-brick floors, wood, glass, reinforced concrete, and marble. Covering two city blocks, the cathedral can accom-modate 2,400 worshippers, seated on three sides of the altar. The modern organ, built in Padua, Italy, counterpoints the architectural innovations; it has 4,842 pipes.

Pacific Heights

For mansion-watchers, rubber-necking in the Pacific Heights district is more gratifying than in Nob Hill. There's an extraordinary collection of dream houses along Broadway and Vallejo streets built by wealth and well endowed with good taste. Architectural features, down to the window shutters and doorknobs, are as original as the flowerbeds and the shrubbery. Many of the fine Edwardian and Victorian homes have remained in private hands, while others function as schools, museums, or consulates.

One of the advantages of living in Pacific Heights is the ready availability of wide-open spaces for walking the dog, playing tennis, or gazing at the skyline. Covering four blocks with trees, flowers, and grass, **Lafayette Park** is the highest of the area's hilltop parks. Another treat afforded by this charmed summit is a superior view of Alcatraz (see page 38) — just behind the **Spreckels Mansion,** built by one of the sugar barons. Modesty has never entered the picture here, and the house might be mistaken as an impressive neo-classical bank or opera house. To their credit, however, the Spreckels were extremely generous patrons of the arts.

Another mansion full of character is the **Haas-Lilienthal House** at 2007 Franklin Street, dating from 1886. Its design is a conglomeration of geometrical shapes — triangles, cones, cubes, and cylinders. Although it is now occupied by the Foundation for San Francisco's Architectural Heritage, you can rent the ballroom for private special events.

Alta Plaza is another Pacific Heights hilltop park of note, steeply terraced and with fine views.

Due south, in the Western Addition, keen photographers head for **Alamo Square** for the picture-perfect row of admirably filigreed Victorian houses in the foreground, with the skyscraper skyline and the bay behind.

Haight-Ashbury

The golden age of Haight-Ashbury is long over, but the reputation and the smell of incense lingers on. You'll notice among the passers-by that there's a high percentage of people on another wavelength and way too many panhandling teenagers. Fond memories of Flower Power and the Summer of Love are recalled in the esoteric shops.

Rebels with flowers in their hair took over the district in the 1960s, pursuing noble goals and, on a more individual level, comprehensive hedonism. The world's infatuation with "Hashbury" and its ideals soon cooled, however, and now nostalgia has taken over. Middle-aged ex-hippies, along with children of the "flower children," can be seen window-shopping along **Haight Street,** looking out for handmade sandals, second-hand clothes, psychedelic art, ancient gramophone records, alternative lifestyle books, and organic food.

 ## Golden Gate Park

One of the largest man-made parks in the world unfolds right from the edge of Haight-Ashbury to the Pacific Ocean.

> ## Out of the Dunes
>
> They laughed in 1870 when civil engineer William H. Hall said San Francisco's barren "Outside Lands" could be reclaimed and turned into a botanical celebration. His hand-picked successor, Scottish-born John McLaren, was determined to finish the job — and he was still at it when he died at the age of 93.
>
> **Golden Gate Park,** a vast green monument to the two dreamers, is filled with anglers, archers, baseball players, cyclists, and enthusiasts of sports, nature, and culture. Parking can be difficult, but there's still room for everyone.

Golden Gate Park is by any standard a triumph of landscaping. Drifting dunes have been transformed into an oasis covered with trees and shrubs of every shade of green, flowers that always seem to be in bloom, and lawns that make you want to run barefoot. Recreational activities to suit all ages and tastes are sprinkled liberally across its 1,017 acres (412 hectares), along with first-class cultural attractions.

The **Conservatory of Flowers**, the oldest building in the park, was badly damaged in a storm a few years back and has yet to be repaired. Money is still being raised to bring this copy of London's Kew Gardens Palm House back to its former glory.

Beautifully restored homes line Alamo Square, framed by the city skyline.

The **M.H. de Young Memorial Museum** is a one-stop headquarters for American art, ranging from colonial to contemporary times, from Paul Revere to Mary Cassatt. There are also landscapes and sculptures from the American West, textiles, and furniture.

Next door, the **Asian Art Museum,** based on the Avery Brundage Collection, offers a sampler of exquisite Chinese, Korean, and Japanese bronzes, ceramics, and paintings. The 12th-century Chinese figurines of warriors,

With its manicured shrubs and koi pond, the Japanese Tea Garden is a favorite stop for visitors at Golden Gate Park.

servants, officials, and animals still retain their animation and energy. It will be moving in 2001 (see page 53).

The **California Academy of Sciences,** on the opposite side of the Music Concourse, has something for everyone: live crocodiles, a stuffed grizzly bear, and a merry-go-round for giant fish. If you thought science was too serious, attend an informal talk by a real scientist, or wander into the bizarrely hilarious exhibit of original "Far Side" cartoons by Gary Larson.

Tour buses park near the **Japanese Tea Garden**, a favorite stop on their routes. All the requisite Japanese subtleties are here, from evocative rocks to a lively koi pond and kid-pleasing bridge. The lackluster tea service isn't what it used to be — try the café in the de Young museum.

The Richmond and Sunset

Set on a dramatic promontory overlooking **Seal Rocks**, the haunt of throngs of sea lions and sea-birds, Cliff House is now a bar and restaurant for tourists, with a fine view and mediocre food. Below, you'll find a visitor center, the **Musée Mécanique,** housing dozens of historic relics of penny arcades, and a Camera Obscura, projecting a "live" panorama into a dark room — as eerie an experience today as it was when Leonardo da Vinci got the idea back in the 15th century. Across the road, the eucalyptus, cypress, and pine forests of **Sutro Heights Park** were planted by Adolph Sutro, a German immigrant who became both rich and mayor of San Francisco, in that order.

Ocean Beach offers about 4 miles (6 km) of inviting sand, but no swimming because of the heavy tides. Even wading here is dangerous because of the undertow, but sunbathing and sunset watching remain appealing.

On the landward side of the Great Highway, parallel to Ocean Beach, **San Francisco Zoo,** one of the country's older municipal animal parks, has recently undergone renovation and expansion to become one of America's premier zoological attractions. It's easy to reach by public transport — at the end of the Muni "L Taraval" streetcar line. Among the novelties you'll see snow leopards, penguins, and koalas from Australia.

EXCURSIONS

Within day-trip distance of San Francisco you can experience the most varied scenery and attractions: picturesque harbors, inspiring forests, crashing surf, vineyards as far as the eye can see, and enviable college towns.

When is a day trip too grueling? San Francisco excursion companies advertise one-day return tours that go as far as

Yosemite National Park — more than 16 hours from start to finish. Lake Tahoe is slightly closer. If you are driving, the wine country north of San Francisco makes a relatively easy day trip, although you may enjoy it more if you take it at a leisurely pace, staying at least one night in a country inn for relaxed wine tasting and gourmet dining.

Here are some ideas for feasible excursions, organized or improvised. We start in the East Bay, move to Marin County, visit Wine Country, and then travel southward to South San Francisco and Monterey.

East Bay

Oakland

If Oakland were just a few hours north from its actual location, it would be a major attraction. But as it stands, in the overwhelming shadow of San Francisco (that sensational skyline is visible from the Oakland waterfront), it's only a sideshow. How cruel of Gertrude Stein to have written of Oakland, "There is no there there." The city is worth your while, though, and it gives you an excuse to ride the comfortable, fast BART (Bay Area Rapid Transit) line beneath the bay — among the supreme American achievements in public transport. Alternatively, you can drive over the Bay Bridge.

The BART train deposits you in the City Square shopping zone, with post-modern skyscrapers in view — though Oakland is not really a skyscraper metropolis. The second impression may cool the initial euphoria; Oakland is a big industrial port city with a few enclaves of glamour, including about 60,000 acres (25,000 hectares) of parklands. With a population of nearly 400,000, Oakland shows a rare ethnic fabric. The census counts just under half the inhabitants as African-American, 34 percent

Caucasian, 9 percent Hispanic, and 8 percent Asian and Pacific islanders. All this explains the city's cosmopolitan shopping and eating possibilities.

Oakland takes a breather, however, in wide open spaces at the heart of the city. **Lake Merritt,** a 155-acre (63-hectare) salt-water lake, has been a game refuge since 1870. It is surrounded by gardens, recreational facilities, and colorful modern apartment and office buildings.

Near the south shore of the lake, the low-lying **Oakland Museum** is subtitled the Museum of California. The contents are top-rate, the displays imaginative, the lushly landscaped architecture exciting, and, unusually, admission is free. The history department, on the second level, has engrossing exhibits on subjects as old as prehistoric inscriptions and as recent as the beatnik era and beyond. Here you'll find all you need to know about the California dream — how it was born and evolved, from the Spanish conquistadores to gold miners to Hollywood hopefuls. The **Gallery of California Art,** on the third level, displays over 550 revealing works. Starting with the gold rush, newly arrived artists were fascinated by the California sunshine, the people of several races, the drama of Yosemite, and San Francisco Bay. (The museum is closed on Monday, Tuesday, and principal holidays.)

Finally, **Jack London Square**, named in honor of the author who grew up in Oakland, is a shopping, eating, and strolling complex on the shore of the estuary. The seafood restaurants enjoy appetizing views of the busy bay and the San Francisco skyline. For historical interest, a primitive cabin on show here is identified as the one Jack London lived in when he followed the gold rush to the Yukon. The First and Last Chance Bar, a few steps away, is said to have been a London haunt. Just in case you think you've had too much to drink, it's

the bar that's tilting; it was salvaged from an old whaler. A floating historic monument is the restored yacht *Potomac,* moored along here, which served as President Franklin Roosevelt's official pleasure craft. After Roosevelt's death, the yacht suffered its ups and downs — Elvis Presley once owned it, and it later sank at Treasure Island.

Berkeley

The brainiest place in the West is the University of California at Berkeley. If a bright idea really did glow like the light bulb in comic strips, this campus would look like the Great White Way.

For a bird's-eye view of the city skyline and the bay, check out Campanile Tower in Berkeley.

With over 30,000 top-flight students and a faculty that includes a galaxy of Nobel prize-winners, Berkeley can permit itself a swagger of pride and a jot of eccentricity.

Interest in the Athens of the Pacific focuses not on the city of Berkeley (notable for its bookstores and gourmet restaurants), but on the campus within, a spacious monument to California's endeavor for academic excellence. Start at the **Student Union** building, where a visitor center supplies maps and information. They also offer guided tours of the campus, but you don't really have to wander far from the Union to get the feeling of student life, with all its passions and fashions.

For a global vantage point, take the elevator (for a small sum) up **Sather Tower,** otherwise known as the Campanile, with a 12-bell carillon. It is 307 ft (94 m) tall and modeled on the one in the Piazza San Marco in Venice. From the top the view puts the town and campus into perspective and offers a bird's eye view of San Francisco, the skyline, and the bay.

Just west of the Campanile, the **Bancroft Library** has exhibits of rare books and manuscripts as well as what's billed as the actual nugget that set off the gold rush.

Stadium Rim Road leads to Strawberry Canyon, where you can enjoy roaming the restful yet scientifically significant **Botanical Gardens**. Beyond, the **Lawrence Hall of Science** honors Ernest Lawrence, the first Berkeley professor to win the Nobel Prize (in 1939) and the developer of the cyclotron. The building is more than a physics laboratory; it's a sort of hands-on science fair for children and adults who want to come to grips with the long and the short of science, from astronomy to biology. (Admission is charged.)

The **Hearst Museum of Anthropology** in Kroeber Hall has unusual exhibits on the cultures of several continents. Closer to home, there are artifacts from the last California Indian tribesman to come into contact with modern society — Ishi — who eluded the white man until 1911, when he came in from the wild.

Across Bancroft Way, the **University Art Museum** has been described as an interpretation of New York's coiled Guggenheim — with corners. Angular spiral ramps are tilted to supersede stairs in a stark concrete interior, which is used to host traveling exhibitions. There are 11 galleries and a sculpture garden.

Telegraph Avenue, a landmark of the counter-culture, is as nonconformist as a barefoot snake-charmer. Here the equally rebellious children of the protest generation dress more or less

as their peacenik parents when Berkeley spawned the radical student movement that swept through the United States in the 1960s, struggling for free speech and against the Vietnam War.

Squatting on the sidewalks, young people today meditate, sell weird earrings and other trinkets, tell your fortune, or hand out leaflets about causes they consider just as urgent as their ancestors' crusades. This is still the perfect place to organize an insurrection.

Marin County

Observe Mother Nature at her finest — whale-watching from atop Point Reyes Lighthouse.

You can also take an even bigger boat, a public ferry, from San Francisco to Sausalito, a half-hour trip. If you drive across the Golden Gate Bridge instead, the views are thrilling, but parking in Sausalito verges on the impossible.

During World War II Sausalito prospered, producing Liberty ships on an assembly line. Now one of these abandoned industrial structures houses the San Francisco Bay-Delta Tidal Hydraulic Model, **Bay Model** for short. Covering 1 acre (0.4 hectares), the computerized model simulates the tides. The US Army Corps of Engineers runs tours.

Tiburon, a pleasant harbor town that can be reached by ferryboat, capitalizes on its wonderful views of the San

Francisco skyline. In the foreground is **Angel Island**, long used for military purposes but now a state park. At Tiburon's ferry slip is Main Street, a little shopping artery full of character. Follow it around the bend to Ark Row, where you can see pretty houseboats which have been beached and converted into shops.

One of California's most distinguished buildings is visible from Highway 101 north of San Rafael. The blue-domed **Marin County Civic Center**, a vast hilltop project, was the last work designed by Frank Lloyd Wright. This brilliantly landscaped experiment houses all manner of facilities, from theaters and the county library to the hall of justice.

If you have time for only one brief whiff of California wilderness, try to make it **Muir Woods National Monument,** a mere 12 miles (19 km) north of the Golden Gate Bridge. The park's 6 miles (10 km) of nature trails offer a sense of tranquillity in the shade of the timeless Coast Redwood trees *(Sequoia sempervirens)*. The aroma of the ancient forest is an elixir for the lungs and the spirit. The trees here — the oldest of which is a thousand years old — are 250 ft (76 m) tall and 14 ft (4 m) thick. The furrows in their bark, like the wrinkles in an old face, seem to attest to all they have survived. The woods are named in honor of the Scottish-born conservationist John Muir (1838–1914).

Another gorgeous spot is the **Point Reyes National Seashore.** The coastline here is so rugged and the surf is so violent that the leaflet and map available at the Bear Valley Visitor Center is full of warnings like "Don't go near the water" and "No life guard on duty." From December to April, whale-watchers mount the observation platform of the **Point Reyes Lighthouse,** which overlooks a notorious graveyard for ships. The famous San Andreas Fault, source of all those earthquakes, separates this peninsula from the mainland, and you can visit the **Earthquake Trail**, near the Visitor Center, which points out traces of the 1906 disaster.

Wine Country

The most crowded time to visit the vineyards north of San Francisco is during the grape harvest, in September or October. All year round, however, the beauty of this region is striking, the eating, drinking, and shopping are absorbing, and the wine tasting is as serious or haphazard as you want. Serious wine buffs will find literature at local tourist offices, in bookshops, and at the wineries, but here is a glance at what's in store, and where.

☞ *Napa Valley*

The scenery of America's most famous wine-growing region, Napa County looks like Spain at its most beautiful — rolling

hills of grapevines and grazing land, eucalyptus, haughty palms and cedars, and flowers alongside the road. You can tour Napa Valley by coach, car, or bicycle, by luxurious vintage train, or from the perspective of a glider or hot-air balloon.

The valley begins at the town of **Napa,** with a population of more than 65,000. A neat and pleasant county

Muir Woods — tranquillity, open air, and timeless shade — an elixir for the spirit.

seat with an ably staffed visitors' center in the central pedestrian area, this is the place to check in for maps, leaflets, and suggestions on accommodation, eating, and wine tasting. In the summer and on weekends, the hotels fill quickly as do the more popular restaurants, so advanced reservations are a good idea.

Northward, the small town of **Yountville** moved into big-time tourism when its giant old winery and distillery were converted into a shopping-and-eating complex, Vintage 1870. Among the nearby wineries are the French-run Domaine Chandon, for sparkling wine; Robert Mondavi, the last word in computerized wine making; and Inglenook-Napa Valley, with tastings in the hundred-year-old heart of the modern operation. Farther afield you'll find the Hess Collection, a Swiss art lover's contemporary museum and winery.

St. Helena is a delightful small town which was smart enough to resist "progress" — at least on the 1890s-style

---

Let There Be Wine

The Spanish padres who founded missions throughout California were the first to grow grapes here; they needed wine, if only for sacramental purposes. But serious commercial production began in the Sonoma Valley in 1857, thanks to a colorful, wine-loving Hungarian nobleman.

With many varieties of cuttings he imported from Europe, Count Agoston Haraszthy established the Buena Vista Winery, which is still in operation. He also founded something of an international dynasty. The count's two sons, niftily named Arpad and Attila, married the daughters of the region's Mexican commander, General Mariano Guadalupe Vallejo, simultaneously, at the Sonoma Mission. Count Haraszthy eventually vanished in Nicaragua.

main street (the local ironmonger does go in for antiques these days). Just north of town you'll find Beringer Vineyards, founded in 1876, and Christian Brothers, where the monks' traditions are still followed in a stone winery.

Since the mid-19th century **Calistoga** has been somewhere for "taking the waters" — and subsequently the wines as well. California's first millionaire, publisher and banker Sam Brannan, bought the land and capitalized on the natural springs. He had planned to name the place Saratoga, after a fashionable spa back east, but during a drinking bout he announced, "We'll make this place the Calistoga of Sarafornia." He died in poverty, but Calistoga flourishes with its volcanic ash mud baths and rejuvenation facilities. When it comes out of the ground the magic water is boiling hot, but it's also bottled and drunk cold — and sold almost everywhere here.

Among the nearby wineries, the most unconventional is Clos Pegase, which combines startling post-modern architecture, an art collection, and stylish wines. Like much of the Napa Valley, it's aimed at the trendy up-market set.

Closer than Yellowstone National Park, you can see a real Old Faithful Geyser just a few miles north of Calistoga. The 60-ft (18-m) jet of boiling water and vapor shoots out of the ground every 50 minutes. Admission is charged.

Sonoma Valley

Closer to San Francisco than the Napa Valley, and more relaxed about entertaining city slickers, the Sonoma Valley offers generous helpings of history along with fine wine.

Sonoma, a captivating town and the county seat, is just how American small towns used to look, with everyone congregating for a chat in the shade of the main square, diagonal parking along its side, and chickens marching about the

Fine wine, sumptuous food, tons of shops, and balmy year-round weather — if it's not heaven, it must be Napa Valley.

lawn. Much aware of its charms, Sonoma nevertheless manages to maintain its modesty.

The main square, **Sonoma Plaza,** covers 8 acres (3 hectares) — vast even by California standards. It contains the city hall, the tourist office, and a duck pond. History was made here in 1846, as a monument in the square recounts, when the flag of the California Republic was first raised. This was a grass-roots American revolt against Mexican rule, which was overtaken by events less than a month later. The Bear Flag is now the official flag of the state of California.

Northeast of the plaza, the San Francisco **Solano Mission,** founded in 1823, is the northernmost of the 21 California missions. The paintings in the adobe church were done by Indian parishioners.

Other buildings around the square include a Mexican army barracks, 19th-century hotels, and historic homes which are now shops and restaurants. Nearby is the house built by General Vallejo, American-Victorian-Gingerbread in style, and quite possibly the most un-Mexican house in the whole of California. He called it "Lachryma Montis," the Latin translation of the original Indian name for this area — "crying mountain."

The wine trail starts within the Sonoma city limits. The Sebastiani Vineyards, producing everything from serious vintages to jugs of popular wines, has tours and tastings. Just outside town is Buena Vista, which maintains a tasting room at 18000 Old Winery Road. Ravenswood, a producer of Zinfandels, at 18701 Gehricke Road, offers tours, tastings, and barbecues.

Glen Ellen Winery, in the district of the same name, and the nearby Valley of the Moon Winery also have tasting facilities. Farther on is the Beauty Ranch, now the **Jack London State Historic Park**, a memorial to the best-selling author of *Call of the Wild* and *The Sea Wolf*. The House of Happy Walls, now a museum, was built by London's widow after he died in 1916. On display are souvenirs he picked up in the South Pacific, his typewriters and eyeshades, and even his first rejection slips. Literary pilgrims from many countries come to see the museum, and hike to London's grave on a nearby hill.

South of San Francisco

Two main highways run southeastward down the San Francisco peninsula. By the bay, Interstate 101, linking the city with the airport, can be as jammed and intimidating as one of the Los Angeles freeways. Somewhat less stressful, and definately more picturesque, is the inland route,

Interstate highway 280 (or the Junípero Serra Freeway), with a scenery bonus of dramatic mountainous countryside.

Just by the Edgewood Road exit of I-280, you can visit the stately home of **Filoli,** with 16 acres (6.5 hectares) of formal gardens — as seen on the television series *Dynasty*. "Filoli" may sound Italian, but it's an acronym for Fight, Love, Live. It was the motto of the owner of the estate, William Bourn, who inherited a gold-rush fortune and parlayed it to even greater wealth as owner of San Francisco's water supply and the head of the gas company. The gardens, improved over more than half a century, have something in bloom most of the year. Tours are operated from Tuesday to Saturday, mostly between February and November. To obtain admission details and make reservations, Tel. (650) 364-2880.

Sonoma Valley combines small town America with the historic west, local shops, and plush vineyards, for genuine family fun.

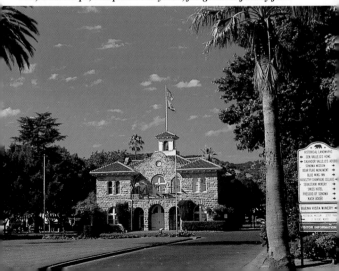

Palo Alto looks like everybody's idea of a small city in contemporary America, a model that is not often seen outside the movies. In the real world of traffic jams, junk-food joints, and litter, it's hard to match the tranquil tree-shaded charm and easy-going pace of University Avenue and the intersecting streets. Palo Alto is a college town, home of a rich, famous, and academically distinguished private university.

Founded in 1885 by the railroad tycoon Leland Stanford, **Stanford University** occupies a dream campus so vast you need a bus, a bike, or a car to get around. It covers 8,180 acres (3,310 hectares) from the Santa Clara Valley to the foothills of the Santa Cruz Mountains. An avenue of stately palms leads from town to the center of campus, the cloistered Main Quadrangle, whose architecture is described as a mixture of Romanesque and Mission Revival.

The tallest and most striking building on campus, the **Hoover Tower**, honors an alumnus, US President Herbert Hoover. The tower and neighboring buildings house the Hoover Institution on War, Revolution and Peace, where great political thinkers have researched and deliberated both during and after the Cold War. From the top of the tower (admission charged) you can see the expanse of Mediterranean-style tile roofs that begins on campus and stretches out as far as the sea.

Admirers of beautiful college campuses should continue from Silicon Valley to **Santa Cruz**, where a redwood forest hides the Santa Cruz division of the state-run University of California system. For its landscape and modern architecture, UCSC, which opened in 1966, is a dynamic endeavor. But there's more than intellectual activity hereabouts. The city of Santa Cruz itself, down the hill, has a 1-mile- (1.6-km-) long swimming beach and an old-fashioned boardwalk with vintage amusement park.

Monterey Peninsula

A scenic three-hour drive south of San Francisco brings you to the Monterey Peninsula, a happy convergence of history, charm, and some of the world's most astounding seascapes. Thanks to the work of conservationists, lobbyists, and far-sighted politicians, the sea lions and seabirds enjoy an unthreatened life along the cliffs and beaches, cypress forests thrive on the ocean breezes, and the towns remain eminently desirable. Despite several million tourists who swoop in every year, high standards are maintained.

The peninsula's principal city, **Monterey**, was the capital of Spanish, Mexican, and briefly, American California, until the gold rush shifted attention to San Francisco. The hilltop **Presidio** of Monterey, the first of the Spanish fortresses founded in California, serves to this day as a

With its endless swimming beach, old-fashioned boardwalk, and vintage amusement park — make way for Santa Cruz!

United States Army base — home of the Defense Language Institute, where military interpreters are trained. Also in Monterey is another elite military institution, the US Naval Postgraduate School.

Crowds of vacationers spend time on **Fisherman's Wharf**, with its cheery boardwalk atmosphere, seafood restaurants, and souvenir shops. Bay sightseeing boats, whale-watching tours (from mid-December until March), and deep-sea fishing expeditions all leave from here. Note the adobe **Custom House**, built in 1814. It was here that the American flag was first raised in California, in 1846.

Legend leads most visitors to Monterey's **Cannery Row**, immortalized by John Steinbeck in his 1945 novel of the same name. However, it has all been spruced up and rather fictionalized since those noisy, smelly, eccentric days. The

With breathtaking seascapes, plentiful wildlife, shops, and more — there's a million reasons to make Monterey a must!

derelict sardine canneries and related structures have been regenerated for the tourism business, and are now art galleries, shopping malls, amusements, and even a wax museum featuring characters from Steinbeck's novels.

The top tourist attraction in town is the **Monterey Bay Aquarium**. Many millions of dollars and all the best ideas in aquarium design and presentation were channeled into this institution, which was inaugurated in 1984. There are light-hearted explanations of all the phenomena of the sea, which mainly focus on the rich local scene. Monterey Canyon, just offshore, is the undersea equivalent of Arizona's Grand Canyon — it's nearly 2 miles (3 km) deep! Children of all ages will enjoy the "touching pool," which includes bat rays, a type of sting ray (but they don't sting). Meanwhile, delightful sea otters frolic both inside and outside the aquarium.

The little-frequented town of **Pacific Grove**, founded by Methodists in 1875, has an incomparable collection of Victorian cottages and a very beautiful public golf course. In addition, gulls, pelicans, cormorants, and other sea-birds in transit haunt the lovely coastline, and millions of Monarch butterflies winter here.

Seventeen-Mile Drive is so spectacular that people pay to see what lies beyond the toll booth. This is also California's golf capital, home of the exclusive Pebble Beach course.

Luxury typifies the small town of **Carmel-by-the-Sea,** the stomping ground of some well-to-do Bohemians. Here you'll find a tremendous range of art galleries, boutiques, and fashionable restaurants. At the end of the main street's incline, a seemingly endless beach of white sand begins. Carmel's 18th-century mission was the favorite of the mission system's founder, Father Junípero Serra, who is buried here.

Museums

Ansel Adams Center for Photography. 250 Fourth Street; Tel. (415) 495-7000. Daily 11am–5pm; adults $5, students $3, seniors/children 3–13 $2.

Asian Art Museum. Golden Gate Park; Tel. (415) 379-8801. Tues–Sun 9:30am–5pm; adults $7, seniors $5, children 12–17 $4, under 12 free. Admission includes same-day entry to the de Young museum.

California Academy of Sciences. Golden Gate Park; Tel. (415) 750-7145. Daily 9am–6pm Memorial Day-Labor Day; 10am–5pm Labor Day–Memorial Day; adults $8.50, seniors/students 12–17 $5.50, children 4–11 $2, under 4 free. Free the first Wednesday of the month.

California Palace of the Legion of Honor. Lincoln Park; Tel. (415) 750-3600. Tues–Sun 9:30am–5pm; adults $8, seniors over 65 $6, children 12–17 $5, under 12 free. Admission is free the second Wednesday of each month. Admission includes same-day entry to the de Young and Asian art museums.

Chinese Historical Society. 964 Clay Street; Tel. (415) 391-1188. Monday 1–4pm, Tues–Fri 10:30am–4pm. Free.

Exploratorium. Bay and Lyon streets; Tel. (415) 561-0360. Daily 10am–5pm summer; closed on Mondays during the school year; adults $9, seniors over 65 $7, children 6–17 $5, 3–5 $2.50.

Jewish Museum. Jewish Community Federation Building, 121 Steuart Street; Tel. (415) 543-8880. Sun–Wed 11am–5pm, Thurs until 8pm; adults $4, seniors/students $2, under 12 free; free first Mon of each month and on Thurs evenings from 6–8pm.

M.H. de Young Memorial Museum. Golden Gate Park; Tel. (415) 863-3330. Tues–Sun 9:30am–5pm; adults $7, seniors $5, children 12–17 $4, under 12 free. Admission is free the first Wednesday of each month. Admission includes entry to the Asian art museum.

San Francisco Museum of Modern Art. 151 Third Street (near Yerba Buena Gardens); Tel. (415) 357-4000. Thurs

11am–9pm, Fri–Tues 11am–6pm, closed Weds and major holidays; adults $9, seniors $6, students $5, children 12 and under free; free first Tuesday of each month and half price Thursday evenings 6–9pm.

San Francisco Maritime National Historic Park. Foot of Polk Street; Tel. (415) 556-3002. Daily 10am–5pm; free.

Wells Fargo History Museum. 420 Montgomery Street;Tel. (415) 396-2619. Mon–Fri 9am–5pm; free.

Attractions

Alcatraz Island. Pier 41 (Fisherman's Wharf); Tel. information: (415) 773-1188, tickets: (415) 705-5555. Daily 9:15am–4:15pm summer, until 2:15pm winter; adults $12.25, seniors 62 and over $10.50, children 5–11 $7.

Coit Tower. Atop Telegraph Hill; Tel. (415) 362-0808. Daily 10am–6pm; admission to the top of the tower: adults $3.75, seniors $2.50, children 6–12 $1.50.

Hyde Street Pier. Foot of Hyde Street at Beach Street; Tel. (415) 556-3002. Daily 9:30am–5pm; adults $4, children 12–17 $2, under 11 free, half-price in winter.

Haas-Lilienthal House. 2007 Franklin Street; Tel. (415) 441-3004. One-hour tours are given Wednesdays from noon to 3pm and Sundays from 11am–4pm; adults $5, seniors 65 and over and children under 12 $3.

Lombard Street. Lombard between Hyde and Leavenworth streets. This residential street is bordered by gardens and the sidewalk is graded to make it easier for walkers.

Mission Dolores. 16th and Dolores streets; Tel. (415) 621-8203. Daily 9am–4pm; adults $2, children 5–12 $1.

Names Project Visitor's Center, 2362A Market Street; Tel. (415) 863-1966. Daily noon–5pm; free.

San Francisco Zoo, Sloat Blvd. and 45th Avenue; Tel. (415) 753-7080. Daily 10am–5pm; adults $9, seniors and children 12–15 $6, children 3–11 $3.

WHAT TO DO

ENTERTAINMENT

From grand opera and avant-garde theater to seedy strip shows, clangorous alternative music clubs, or languorous cocktail lounges, every aspect of entertainment is available in San Francisco, a noted good-time town. Particular kinds of entertainments seem to cluster in neighborhoods: Try Nob Hill for a sentimental piano bar, North Beach for the blues or a raunchy review, Union Square for theater, Civic Center for culture. In addition, you'll find congenial haunts with singular ethnic, musical, or social orientation spread all over town.

For a preview of coming attractions, turn to the Internet if handy, and investigate newspaper web sites <www.sfgate.com/eguide> or <www.sfbg.com>, or the city guide <bayarea.citysearch.com>. Once in town, consult the encyclopedic survey of what's on in the pink "Datebook" section of the whopping Sunday edition of the *San Francisco Chronicle* or study a copy of the *Bay Guardian*, a giveaway weekly easily found in bookstores, cafés, and in sidewalk kiosks.

If too much pre-planning removes all the excitement of an evening out, meander down to the TIX counter on the east side of Union Square. Here, tickets for certain shows are available at half price, starting at noon on the day of the performance only. (TIX also sells full-price tickets for future performances. It's closed Sunday and Monday.)

Opera, ballet, classical music: War Memorial Opera House (Van Ness Avenue at Grove Street), in the shadow of City Hall, is one of the most glamorous venues for an evening out. The gala season of the San Francisco Opera company (Tel. 415-864-3330) runs from September to December, followed by a season of the San Francisco Ballet (Tel. 415-865-2000) on the same stage from February until June. Elsewhere, many ethnic and experimental dance companies perform at almost any time of year.

Across the street from the Opera House is the modern Louise M. Davies Symphony Hall, where the San Francisco Symphony Orchestra (Tel. 415-864-6000) holds forth between September and July. The interior design is elegant, the acoustics controversial.

For less formal concerts, enjoy chamber music, piano and violin duos, or classical-

Fisherman's Wharf is always groovin' with countless local artists and performers.

ly trained singers at Old First Presbyterian Church on Sacramento Street at Van Ness Avenue (Tel. 415-474-1608). Tickets are modestly priced and the cable car will take you to within two blocks of the church. Over the summer, a great variety of music is available free on Sunday afternoons at Stern Grove, in the woods at Sloat Boulevard and 19th Avenue. Another local secret is the schedule of free concerts offered at the music store Star Classics (425 Hayes Street; Tel. 415-552-1110) Fridays at noon and Sundays at 5pm.

Theater and cinema: Among dozens of local live theater groups, the American Conservatory Theater (415 Geary Street. Tel. 415-749-2228) has acquired the widest national reputation. Its repertory season runs from October until June. Broadway hits appear next door at the Curran Theater or a few blocks away at the Golden Gate Theater and Orpheum. All three venues share the same telephone number (Tel. 415-551-2000). In summer there's free Shakespeare in Golden Gate Park.

Turning to films: First-run movies, art house cinema, and classics are shown all over the city, especially in multiplexes along Van Ness Avenue, in Japantown, at the Embarcadero Center, and south of Market in the Metreon. The Castro Theater, an art deco movie palace built in the 1920s on Castro Street, is often the spot for interesting documentaries and film festival favorites.

Pop and rock: Nightclubs, auditoriums, and music bars all over town cover the musical waterfront with live performances of contemporary rock music, jazz, blues, and funk. The SoMa District is also a hotbed of alternative music, but the scene stretches from Union Square to, of all places, Fisherman's

Swinging in Ghirardelli Square — live music, shops, galleries, and then some...

Wharf. If you want to dance to salsa or other Latin rhythms, swing by Mission District clubs such as Roccapulco (Tel. 415-648-6611).

Jazz: When big jazz names visit the area they tend to perform across the bay at Yoshi's in Oakland (Tel. 510-238-9200). In North Beach, Jazz at Pearl's (Tel. 415-291-8255) features a Monday Big Band night and local musicians Tuesday–Saturday.

Comedy and cabaret: San Francisco has a big sense of humor, and local comedy clubs have hatched the talents of many well-known personalities, including Whoopi Goldberg and local resident Robin Williams. Cobb's Comedy Club at the Cannery (Tel. 415-928-4320) holds a Monday night marathon and regular shows the rest of the week. The Punchline (444 Battery Street; Tel. 415-397-7573) hosts nationally known and local talent nightly except Mondays. On the cabaret front, see who's playing the Plush Room (940 Sutter Street; Tel. 415-885-2800), the preferred stage for torch singers. In North Beach a gloriously silly satirical musical review, *Beach Blanket Babylon*, has been packing them in for over two decades; adults only except for Sunday matinees. Call far ahead for tickets to these immensely popular shows; Tel. (415) 421-4222.

SHOPPING

Like the city itself, shopping in San Francisco is stylish, cosmopolitan, and innovative. Here you will find whatever you've been looking for, including fashions, fads, and gadgets you never knew you needed.

Don't limit yourself to department stores or malls, where the retailers all look alike. San Francisco is full of old-fashioned neighborhoods where gourmet food markets vie for attention with ultra-cool clothing boutiques, gift shops, and bookstores. While an influx of chain stores has diminished the local color of shopping blocks here and there, every neighborhood has a number of unique stores that reflect the taste and passions of their owners.

When to Shop

Hours vary from shop to shop and district to district, but the department stores operate from 9:30 or 10am to 8pm Monday–Friday, till 6 or 7pm Saturday, and from noon to 6pm on Sunday. Note that some smaller shops close on Sunday.

Where to Shop

The place to start for a survey of San Francisco shopping is **Union Square,** which manages to pack in more exclusive retailing than almost any other area. The nationally famous department stores are here, along with elegant boutiques down the nearby lanes. Also downtown is the **San Francisco Shopping Centre,** at Market and Fifth streets, a 9-story vertical shopping mall.

SoMa (South of Market), especially techno-savvy South Park between 2nd and 4th, Bryant, and Brannan treets, holds treasures in fashion and home decor. Discount outlets also abound in the neighborhood; for a good resource on outlet shopping pick up a copy of *Bargain Hunting in the Bay Area* by Sally Socolich.

Historic **Jackson Square,** on the edge of the Financial District, specializes in pricey antiques displayed in appropriately antique surroundings.

Chinatown is a seething bazaar where the choice of exotica is overwhelming — from an abacus to X-rated fortune cookies.

With over 100 specialty shops, restaurants, and guided tours, there's no wonder why Pier 39 keeps packing them in.

Embarcadero Center — like Chinatown, another city-within-the-city — is an urban redevelopment project similar in scale to the Rockefeller Plaza in New York, with more than 150 shops among the offices, restaurants, cafés, sculptures, and bright flower-filled pots.

North Beach, birthplace of the beatniks, specializes in offbeat shops and genuinely interesting bookshops, including the famous City Lights. Also eccentric is **Haight Street,** the main thoroughfare of the one-time flower-power Haight-Ashbury district, with nostalgia rampant in the shops.

Union Street, an area of Victorian-era houses, has since been upgraded into a smart shopping zone of stylish boutiques, accessories for home and body, and lots of restaurants. Same for **Fillmore Street,** which contains some only-in-San-Francisco gems.

Fisherman's Wharf is geared strictly toward tourists with sweatshirt emporiums and dubious art that lines Jefferson Street and spills into **Pier 39**. A better choice is **Ghirardelli Square,** a 19th-century factory complex overlooking the bay, which has been converted into a tasteful array of shops, galleries, and restaurants. **The Cannery** also has three floors of shops, cafés, and attractions in an 1890s former peach cannery across the street.

What to Buy

San Francisco is a great place to shop for art, high-quality crafts, clothing, items for the home, and wine. Be sure to browse offbeat galleries and gift shops where many local artists provide everything from funky jewelry and handbags fashioned from antique kimonos to découpaged and hand-painted furniture.

With the second largest Chinese community outside of Asia, Chinatown lets you visit Asia without leaving the country.

Books: Writing, reading, and publishing books are venerable traditions in San Francisco: Dashiell Hammett, Jack London, Jack Kerouac, and Mark Twain all have their own local connections.

Clothing: In a fashion capital like San Francisco you face an embarrassment of riches, but sportswear and casual styles are a good bet. Blue jeans fans should check out the new Levi's store on Union Square where customers can personally soak themselves and their new jeans in a "shrink-to-fit" tank.

Food and drink: Sourdough bread is wrapped "to go" at the airport — handy if you've a long wait. Also, San Francisco chocolates, candies, and salami make good portable souvenirs. Or why not take home a bottle of fine California wine?

Gadgets: There will always be something new and fascinating for the kitchen, car, or office to be found in San Francisco. If it's electrical, though, make sure the equipment can be adapted to the voltage back at home.

Sporting goods: It's worth pricing the golf and tennis equipment, and don't forget to take home a baseball cap.

Toys: Children are well catered to in San Francisco. Both big and little shops sell the latest in toys, games, and educational gifts.

SPORTS

Never too hot, never too cool, the climate encourages sporting people of many disciplines to excel year round. Only the swimming can be problematic. The beaches may be beautiful, but the tides are treacherous, the water cold, and the fog can cast a pall.

Golf: There are six public courses, including the 18-hole Presidio green opened to the public in 1995 (Tel. 415-561-4653). For golf as well as inspiring views, try out the Lincoln Park (Tel. 415-750-GOLF) or Harding Park (Tel. 415-664-4690) courses. If you've come to California for the golfing experience of your life, Pebble Beach is less than 3 hours by car south of San Francisco.

Tennis: There are over 100 well-maintained tennis courts in parks around San Francisco that are city-run and free — first come, first served. (The courts at Dolores Park on Dolores and 18th Street are lighted at night.) A fee is charged for the 21 courts in Golden Gate Park. At the top end of the market, the San Francisco Tennis Club at 645 Fifth Street (Tel. 415-777-9000) has indoor and outdoor courts as well as exercise facilities.

Rainy Day Pastimes

San Francisco weather is usually mild, but in case wind, rain, or fog make outdoor activities too chilling, there are fine indoor alternatives. The five-story Sony Metreon at Yerba Buena Gardens is filled with activities, including 15 movie theaters, numerous restaurants, a virtual games room and shopping opportunities. Museums are also perfect havens during wet weather, especially the Museum of Modern Art on Third Street or the California Academy of Science in Golden Gate Park. A thorough look through the exhibits can be followed by a bite to eat and a stroll through the gift shop. Around Union Square, the Rotunda restaurant at Neiman Marcus, and the Sheraton Palace and Westin St. Francis hotels all serve afternoon tea in lovely surroundings.

*For a respite from exploring the city, take to the beach,
where you can ride the tide or stroll the coast.*

Cycling: Yet another San Francisco advantage, with all the
scenic surroundings available. There are two bike routes:
one through Golden Gate Park to the Great Highway, the
other from the southern part of the city to the Golden Gate
Bridge. Rental shops are to be found alongside the park.

Jogging: Golden Gate Park is a favorite, but you might also
like to experience the peace and tranquillity of the 5-mile
path around Lake Merced, or the bay views from the Marina
Green, or parallel the Pacific on Ocean Beach. Serious long-
distance runners can compete in the San Francisco
Marathon, or the costume optional Bridge to Bridge Run.

Hiking: There are many beautiful hiking trails on Mt. Tam
across the bay in Marin, but you don't have to leave the city
to break in your boots. For views and a challenging walk,
take the **Coastal Trail** from Fort Point (underneath the

Golden Gate Bridge) to the Cliff House; but don't climb on the cliffs themselves, as they aren't stable. Eight miles from the shore, **Angel Island** sports a dozen miles of trails; ride the Blue and Gold Ferry and take a picnic lunch.

Boating: For bay boating, with or without a licensed captain, see the charter firms along the Embarcadero or in Sausalito. The Blue and Gold fleet (Tel. 415-773-1188) has regularly scheduled one-hour bay cruises that motor under the Golden Gate Bridge and pass Alcatraz and Angel islands. Other firms combine dining with sailing, including The Ruby (Tel. 415-861-2165) and Hornblower Dining Yachts (Tel. 415-788-8866).

Fishing: Several deep-sea fishing companies operate out of Fisherman's Wharf. The boats leave very early in the morning in search of salmon, bass, or whatever is running. If sea-

If you need an escape from the throngs of tourists on the pier, Aquatic Park has plenty of beach for the whole family.

sickness is a problem, you might prefer casting a line from Municipal Pier in Aquatic Park.

Spectator Sports

Baseball: One of the great American pastimes unfolds, slowly, at the spiffy new Pacific Bell Park, when the San Francisco Giants are in town. Seating is limited to 40,000, so tickets may be difficult to come by. Across the bridge, the A's play at the Oakland Coliseum.

Basketball: Big-time basketball takes over after the baseball season ends. The Golden State Warriors of the National Basketball Association's Pacific Division entertain in Oakland Coliseum.

Football: Named after the gold rush invaders, the powerful San Francisco '49ers of the National Football League are based at 3Com Park at Candlestick Point. The season runs from August to December. Tickets are nearly impossible to get. The Oakland Raiders are also worth watching, or catch a college game — Stanford University is often one of the nation's top teams.

Horse racing: The nearest thoroughbred racing is held at Golden Gate Fields (Tel. 510-559-7300) in Albany, north of Berkeley off Interstate 80. Twenty minutes south on Highway 101 is Bay Meadows in San Mateo (Tel. 415-574-7223). The horse-racing season takes place all year, alternating between these two fields.

CHILDREN'S SAN FRANCISCO

Frank Sinatra aptly described San Francisco as a "grown-up, swinging town," but it's equally swinging for kids. If anyone

Climb on board the historic ships of Hyde Street Pier for a glimpse into maritime history.

needs an impromptu push, few parks are bereft of play structures, and what child, small or large, would deny the true excitement of a ride on the cable cars?

Since no parent can resist the chance to inculcate his offspring with a little culture, a number of museums will do the trick without resistance. The made-for-children **Exploratorium** (Tel. 415-561-0360) is one of the finest science museums in the world and full of hands-on exhibits of interest to all ages. The **California Academy of Sciences** in Golden Gate Park (Tel. 415-750-7145) hosts traveling exhibits along with enduring animal dioramas and has a nifty aquarium where kids can poke at starfish and sea urchins. The planetarium shows at Morrison Planetarium inside the academy (Tel. 415-750-7141) are also entertaining. Other park attractions include a huge playground and charming carousel. South of Market, **Zeum** (Tel. 415-777-2800) at Yerba Buena Gardens is a fascinating technology center geared toward older kids and teens with an interest in computers, art, and video. Nearby on Fourth Street is the **Cartoon Art Museum** (Tel. 415-227-8666) with exhibits on underground and mainstream comics.

Ice skating and **bowling** are other youthful favorites at Yerba Buena Gardens, and neither require advance reservations. **The Metreon** itself is a kid magnet with its Airtight Garage, interactive video games, movies, and shops. Farther afield, the 65-acre **San Francisco Zoo** (Tel. 415-753-7080) is filled with over 1,000 animals, a zoo train, and a large playground. A visit to Ocean Beach can be combined with a stop at the **Musée Mécanique** below the Cliff House (Tel. 415-386-1170). This small museum is loaded with fantastically restored mechanical toys and games that were the forerunners to pinball and video machines. Bring along a roll of quarters.

Down near **Fisherman's Wharf** and **Aquatic Park** are seaworthy places to spend time with the kids, including inside the WWII submarine *U.S.S. Pampanito* (Tel. 415-441-5819) and the **Hyde Street Pier** (Tel. 415-556-3002), home to a historic ships open for tours. If the weather turns ugly, turn to **The Cannery** where you can create a new stuffed pal at the **Basic Brown Bear Factory** (Tel. 415-931-6670) or paint ceramics at **Handmade Ceramic Studio** (Tel. 415-440-2898).

On the Beaches

If you don't mind brisk temperatures, go ahead and dip your toes in the Pacific Ocean. Here are some sandy beaches, reading from north to south:

Baker Beach, part of the Presidio, is highly unsafe for swimming but popular with joggers, picnickers, and sunbathers (nude ones on the northern portion).

China Beach, also known as Phelan Beach, is a protected cove where swimming is permitted; lifeguards are on duty during the warmer months.

Ocean Beach runs on and on alongside the Great Highway south from the Cliff House. Swimming can be quite dangerous, but the sand and sunsets are superb.

Festivals

Parades, street fairs, and celebrations of the most exotic types occur with great frequency in San Francisco. Some of the highlights to note are:

February–March: Chinese New Year: fireworks, dragon dances, and a parade through Chinatown. St. Patrick's Day parade, downtown. The Martin Luther King Birthday Celebration.

April: Cherry Blossom Festival, Japantown. S.F. International Film Festival, various locations around town.

May: Cinco de Mayo (5 May) Mexican fiesta and parade, Mission District. Carnival (Memorial Day weekend): a wild parade and festival featuring samba dancers, food, crafts, music, Mission District.

June: Gay Freedom Day parade to the Civic Center. Union Street Fair, arts and crafts on Union between Fillmore and Gough Streets. North Beach Festival, the oldest urban street fair, North Beach.

July: Fourth of July fireworks along the waterfront. San Francisco Flower Show in Golden Gate Park. Jazz and All That Art on Fillmore, Fillmore Street between Post and Jackson streets.

August: A La Carte, A La Park: food festival with great music in Golden Gate Park.

September: Blues Festival at Fort Mason, and the renowned Shakespeare festival in Golden Gate Park. Autumn Moon Festival in Chinatown. Festival de las Americas, Mission District.

October: Columbus Day parade, Italian-American Festival in North Beach. Castro Street Fair. Exotic-Erotic Ball on Halloween. Jazz Festival.

November: Day of the Dead Festival, Mission District. Bay Area Book Festival, Fort Mason.

Customs and Coffee

Small-town Americans have dinner as early as 5pm, even when they come to San Francisco, but it's more fashionable to dine after 7pm, and most restaurants stay open to 10pm or later. Breakfast is served from about 7 to about 10am, though in many establishments breakfast specialties such as pancakes and scrambled eggs are served all day long. Lunch is usually served between noon and 2pm.

Coffee appears to be the local drink of choice based on the fact that coffee bars take up more real estate than even Gap clothing stores (which you'll also find on nearly every street corner). Once you order your tall lowfat, no-foam latte with a sprinkle of cocoa, you're on your own. But in restaurants, your waiter will appear with great frequency to inquire if you'd like a refill of java. Thus you may dilute your meal with several cups for the price of one, if caffeine is your thing.

Tipping is straightforward. Before all the taxes have been added to the bill ("the check"), calculate 15 percent of the total and allocate it to the waiter or waitress, up to 20 percent in the case of extraordinary service. In many informal eateries you pay the cashier on the way out, leaving a tip on the table or in a tip jar located on the counter.

Specialties

The big drawing card in San Francisco is the **seafood,** so wholesome that it doesn't take a famous chef to do it justice. **Dungeness Crab** is the local specialty. It is available from mid-November to May and is served in many forms — Newburg, steamed fresh, au gratin, or, less elegantly, as morsels assembled as takeaway snacks in plastic cups. Other shellfish that grace the menu are shrimp, oysters, scallops, and mussels.

One part-seafood dish even comes with its own legend. The wryly named **Hangtown Fry** — scrambled eggs, ham, and oysters — is said to have been devised in gold rush days by a gallows-bound prisoner in Placerville. In his request for a last meal, the wily criminal chose ingredients that would take some time to assemble.

Seafood also figures in many of the ethnic restaurants. **Cioppino,** an Italian-descended seafood stew, is claimed as a San Francisco original. Thai restaurants serve spicy crab salad, Chinese chefs immerse lobster in black bean sauce, and fresh scallops and prawns appear in Japanese *sushi*.

Fresh fish from the broad Pacific is another of San Francisco's advantages. Swordfish, salmon, tuna, and seabass are meaty enough to satisfy even the most deter-

With a rich multi-cultural heritage, San Francisco's local cuisine is guaranteed to satisfy the most courageous palates.

mined carnivore. The giant fish are sliced into steaks, while smaller ones are usually filleted. In the United States, fish are normally served minus heads and tails.

Meat eaters can start with steaks in their all-American diversity — Porterhouse, *filet mignon*, T-bone. Roast beef, veal, lamb, and pork round out the menu. In the meantime, don't underestimate the great American hamburger.

For **vegetarians** California offers a better choice than almost anywhere else. Not only are the ingredients impeccable, but there's an understanding of nutritional requirements. There are a handful of vegetarian eateries in town, and a few achieve gourmet level; almost all local restaurants have creative vegetarian dishes on the menu.

Desserts include some sensational fresh fruits. Pies and cakes are as rich as you can stand them, and the ice-cream, in a truly bewildering array of flavors, is an inspiration. Only a few upscale restaurants have cheeses on the dessert menu, although the list is growing.

California Wine

California's wine-makers have added the advantages of science and technology to an already blessed climate, assuring consistently superior results. Scientists at the University of California at Davis have bred new hybrid grapes with names like Ruby Cabernet and Centurion, designed to upgrade hitherto boring table wines. Visiting wine aficionados will enjoy tracking down world-class vintages. To the ordinary diner, the California revolution simply means that even the least pompous house wine is eminently drinkable. Wine can be ordered by the glass or bottle.

Every sort of wine produced in Europe, from **Sherry** and **Champagne**-style sparkling wine to **Port** and **brandy,** has its equivalent in California — plus Japanese *sake,* distilled from local rice and served in sushi bars and Japanese restaurants.

Labels identify the winery, the region, the variety of grape, the vintage year if appropriate, and alcoholic content. Classic European grapes like Cabernet Sauvignon and Pinot Noir are represented, along with less-familiar hybrids like Gamay Beaujolais. California's vineyards stretch all the way from San Diego county, where the Spanish friars planted the first grapes in 1769, to Mendocino in the cool north.

You don't have to be an expert in varietals and vintages to enjoy forays in the Sonoma and Napa valleys, the wine zones most easily accessible from San Francisco (see pages 69–72). Take advantage of the tastings and tours offered by many of the popular wineries.

Other Drinks

In cosmopolitan San Francisco people drink Scotch whisky or Polish vodka, Irish coffee or Mexican tequila, as well as a

By Bread Alone

You'd have to go to Paris to find a bread remotely as tasty as San Francisco's **sourdough**. Many a tourist carry home souvenir loaves.

What makes sourdough bread so good is the secret ingredient descended from a micro-organism brought from Europe in time for the gold rush. Prospectors carried small quantities of this "starter" of fermented dough to cause the bread they baked in the wilds to rise. A bit of this same bacillus is recycled every day in the complex process used by the bakeries of San Francisco. Sourer or sweeter, darker or lighter, according to your choice, the crusty end-product can be a meal in itself.

Since its days as a chocolate factory, Ghirardelli Square has managed to transform itself into an all-out shopping hotspot.

staggering range of **cocktails.** One of the best perhaps is a **margarita** — iced tequila with Cointreau or Triple Sec, lime juice, and a coating of salt around the rim of the glass.

Beer, domestic or imported, is normally served very cold in glasses or mugs. There are "micro breweries" all over town, where you can admire to gleaming tanks and taste various styles of beer and ale produced on the premises. San Francisco's contribution to the science of beer-making is "steam beer," an historic method of brewing using air cooling rather than ice.

Health faddists, who seem to abound in California, may prefer to sip brand-name mineral waters, perhaps with a sliver of low-calorie lime, or fresh **fruit juices** with a dollop of protein powder blended at specialty juice bars that grace most neighborhoods.

HANDY TRAVEL TIPS

An A–Z Summary of Practical Information

A

ACCOMMODATIONS (see also CAMPING, YOUTH HOSTELS, and the list of Recommended Hotels starting on page 125)

Some of the world's finest and most famous hotels contribute to San Francisco's reputation for hospitality. These exclusive hotels compete on the basis of their international reputations and such "little extras" as discreet concierges, complimentary limousine service, fresh flowers, and twice-daily maid service. One of them (the Westin St. Francis) even runs a "money laundering" operation to be sure all the coins handed to guests are impeccably clean and shiny. Of course, most of the 30,000 hotel rooms on the city's books are more modest, but charm and comfort persist far down the line from the luxury class.

Hotel chains such as the Marriott, Hyatt, and Hilton are well represented, as are more intimate "boutique" hotels and bed-and-breakfast establishments. It's always wise to have advance reservations. Most hotels have toll-free telephone numbers, but keep in mind that they can only be dialed from within the United States.

All hotel rates in San Francisco are subject to a 14 percent room tax. Parking downtown can add another $10 to $25 per day, and telephone surcharges will also inflate the bill.

For a free Lodging Guide published annually by the San Francisco Convention & Visitors Bureau contact the bureau at (800) 220-5747 (toll-free in US) or write them at 900 Market Street, San Francisco, CA 94102.

AIRPORTS

San Francisco International Airport has the auspicious title of the seventh-busiest airport in the world, handling about 1,300 flights per day. The airport is on the freeway 14 miles (23 km) south of the city — half an hour by taxi but a bit longer during the rush hour. A major expansion project, due for completion around 2006, aims to ease the crowding in the efficient but overstretched terminal and will add a BART station. Information booths, with multilingual staff, are located near baggage claim areas in each terminal. No airport or departure taxes are collected from travelers.

Taxis are always available outside the doors of the arrival area. The fare to downtown is around $30 plus tip. Shuttle vans are available at center islands outside the upper-level departure terminals. They provide door-to-door service for $12 per person; advance reservations are not necessary. If you are renting a car, a courtesy bus will deposit you at the new, rather inefficient rental car building where all the rental counters and cars are located.

An alternative to SFO Airport is the less hectic Oakland International Airport across the Bay. A shuttle bus links the airport to the BART rapid transit line (see page 119) to downtown San Francisco. Otherwise, taxis and shuttle buses are available outside the airline terminals.

B

BICYCLE RENTAL

There are miles of agreeable cycling routes in Golden Gate Park, and on Sundays John F. Kennedy Drive is closed to automobile traffic so you can cycle nearly to the beach free of exhaust fumes. Bikes may be hired on Stanyan Street near the park's eastern boundary for around $5 per hour. Cycling across the Golden Gate Bridge is also enjoyable (if windy), and at least one rental company (Bay Bicycle Tours in the Cannery; Tel. 415-923-6434) offers a bike tour to Sausalito with a return trip by ferry. Cycling is a popular way of exploring the wine country north of San Francisco, with rentals and tours available in Sonoma, St. Helena, and Calistoga.

BUDGETING for YOUR TRIP

San Francisco isn't an inexpensive destination. The average daily expenditure per visitor is over $130 according to the Convention &

Visitors Bureau, with the bulk of expenses divided between lodging and food. While many hotels offer weekend and off-season rates, there isn't a true low season in the city.

Accommodations. Plan to pay from $75 for a modest motel room outside Union Square to $185 on up for a small but smartly decorated room at the city's finer boutique hotels. Then add 14% room tax and another $20 or so, per day, if you plan to park a car downtown. Hotels closer to the Tenderloin tend to be less expensive, but if you want to save on accommodations, consider instead places in outlying neighborhoods, such as the Sunset, that are close to public transportation. On the web, <www.bay area.citysearch.com> is a good resource for listings.

Meals. You can eat well without blowing your entire budget although it will be tempting to splurge for at least one superb dinner while you're here. Ethnic restaurants in the Mission District, Chinatown, Japantown, and the Richmond District are generally quite inexpensive and offer a wonderful opportunity to sample cuisines from around the world. You can easily spend under $15 per person for a great Chinese, Mexican, Salvadoran, Vietnamese, Thai, or Japanese meal (among others) by exploring these neighborhoods.

Transportation. Driving a car in the city is an expensive and aggravating proposition. If possible, use public transportation and taxis while inside the city limits. Buses and Muni cost $1 and you'll receive a transfer good for a second trip within 2 hours. Cab fare runs $2 for the first mile then $1.80 per mile. Parking fees are hefty downtown and at Fisherman's Wharf where the major lot charges $5 per hour.

Attractions. Some of the best attractions in town are free, including the Golden Gate Bridge, Chinatown, and Strybing Arboretum in Golden Gate Park. Museum admissions begin at $7 for adults (nearly half for kids), and a daytime tour to Alcatraz will set a couple back almost $25.

C

CAMPING

There are campsites in state parks outside San Francisco in Marin County and Half Moon Bay, but camping is not allowed in the city. For information, write to California Department of Parks and Recreation, Attention Publications Office, PO Box 942896, Sacramento, CA 94296. National Parks Service information is available from Building 201, Fort Mason, San Francisco, CA 94123. For addresses and telephone numbers of commercial campgrounds for recreational vehicles see the *Yellow Pages* under "Campgrounds & Recreational Vehicle Parks."

CAR RENTAL/HIRE

Driving and parking in the city can be an unpleasant experience at best and if you can avoid renting a car, do so. For trips outside the city, rent on an as-needed basis from one of the many firms located around Union Square. Car rental companies compete for business, so it's worth shopping around if you have the time and patience. At the airport and downtown, every national firm is represented (Avis, Budget, Hertz, National) as well as smaller local companies such as Enterprise. Prices vary widely under the laws of supply and demand, according to the season, and even within a single firm on the same day. Look into special weekly and weekend rates and Internet specials, but budget about $40 per day, not including parking fees.

Automatic transmission and air-conditioning are standard. Note that rates which sound reasonable can end up much higher when insurance is added. Check your auto insurance policy to see if you are fully covered for rentals before accepting the "collision damage waiver" option. This insurance will add $10 per day or more to the cost. Also, you'll probably save if you hire a car with unlimited mileage.

Renters need a valid driver's license plus an International Driving Permit if you reside outside the US or Canada. Most agencies set a minimum age for car rental at 25, some at 21 and a credit card is required.

CLIMATE

The biggest surprise for visitors is that summer can be very chilly. Those people shivering in shorts are uninformed tourists. If they had driven an hour inland they might be sweltering in tropical sunshine, but the famous fog transmits cold ocean temperatures into the city. Oddly, the warmest season is autumn. Of course, it doesn't take much to constitute a heat wave in San Francisco. Winters are cold, often rainy, and sometimes windy.

To help you with long-range predictions, here are the average daily maximum and minimum temperatures by month for San Francisco.

	J	F	M	A	M	J	J	A	S	O	N	D
maximum												
°F	55	59	61	62	63	66	65	65	69	68	63	57
°C	13	15	16	17	17	19	18	18	21	20	17	14
minimum												
°F	45	47	48	49	51	52	53	53	55	54	51	47
°C	7	8	9	9	11	11	12	12	13	12	11	8

CLOTHING

A sweater or jacket is likely to be welcome for at least part of every day in San Francisco, even during what the rest of the northern hemisphere knows as summer. Generally, mid-weight clothing is the best bet year-round, though an all-weather coat will come in handy in winter. Comfortable walking shoes go a long way toward taming the hills. Like the rest of California, San Franciscans have succumbed to an informal dress code. The best restaurants require a coat for gentlemen, but casual clothes are acceptable nearly everywhere you go.

COMPLAINTS

If you have a serious complaint about business practices, first talk to the manager of the establishment. Should this fail to resolve the problem, try the Better Business Bureau, 114 Sansome Street, Suite 1103; Tel. (415) 243-9999.

CRIME & SAFETY

With a relatively low crime rate for a large city, San Francisco poses no special dangers. However, the lack of gun control in the US means that in general, criminals are more dangerous. Take cabs late at night, don't walk unescorted in the wee hours, and avoid the mysteries of dark streets or run-down areas. Leave valuables in your hotel safe, and beware of pickpockets in crowded places and on Muni. If you have a car, don't leave anything inside in plain sight and always lock the doors. The all-purpose emergency telephone number is **911.** For less urgent police business, dial (415) 553-0123.

CUSTOMS & ENTRY REQUIRMENTS

For a stay of less than 90 days, British visitors with a valid ten-year passport and a return ticket on a major airline do not generally need a US visa. Nationals of most other European countries are given the same priority. Canadian visitors merely have to show proof of nationality. Citizens of Australia, Portugal, and South Africa need a visa, but rules do change, so check with your local US embassy or consulate, or with your travel agent.

If you do need a visa, application forms are available through travel agents, airlines, or US consulates. Allow at least a month for postal applications. Forms must be accompanied by a passport valid for at least six months longer than the intended visit, a passport-size photo, evidence of possession of sufficient funds, and proof of intent to leave the US after the visit. A health certificate is not normally required.

Red and green channels are in use at America's international airports and all formalities are simpler and quicker than in the past. If you fly in, you should be given the customs and immigration forms to complete well before landing.

Duty-free allowance. The following chart shows certain duty-free items a non-resident may take into the US (if you are over 21) and, when returning home, into your own country.

Into:	Cigarettes		Cigars		Tobacco	Spirits		Wine
US	200	or	50	or	1,350g	1 l	or	1 l
Australia	200	or	250	or	250g	1 l	or	1 l
Canada	200	and	50	and	900g	1.14 l	or	1.14 l
Ireland	200	or	50	or	150g	1 l	and	2 l
New Zealand	200	or	50	or	250g	1.1 l	and	4.5 l
South Africa	400	and	50	and	250g	1 l	and	2 l
UK	200	or	50	or	250g	1 l	and	2 l

A non-resident may take into the US gifts, free of duty and taxes, to a value of $100. The import of plants, seeds, vegetables, fruits, or other fresh food is prohibited; foods of all kinds are subject to inspection. If you're carrying money and checks totaling more than $10,000 in or out of the country, they must be reported.

DRIVING

The United States is the land of the car, but when it comes to San Francisco the best advice is "don't" — except for out-of-town trips. The hills and parking problems exacerbate the normal hazards of city driving.

The regulations are straightforward. Drive on the right, pass on the left. Unless there's a sign to the contrary, you can turn right on a red signal, providing that you stop and check that no pedestrians or traffic deter this maneuver. Drivers and all passengers must wear seatbelts; children under 4 years require child restraints. Cable cars always have the right of way, as do pedestrians at the designated

crosswalks. School buses (painted yellow) are given special priori
by law; it is a serious offense to pass a school bus *in either directic*
on a two-lane road when it is taking on or discharging passengers.

Highways. California has no toll roads, though you have to pay
cross the Golden Gate Bridge or the San Francisco-Oakland B
Bridge. (Fares are collected only as you arrive in San Francisco.) Tl
freeway system is complicated enough to deserve advanced plannin
if you miss an exit you can lose a lot of time trying to double back

Speed limits. On Interstate highways the limit is normally 65 m|
(105 km/h). On all other highways the limit is 55 mph (90 km/h).

Parking. "Curbing" the wheels of a parked car is the law in S;
Francisco, so that if a car rolls downhill the curb will brake
Parking downhill, turn your wheels toward the curb; parking uphi
away from the curb. Engage the handbrake and put the car in ge;
Parking meters govern the time you can stay in some areas and ma;
only accept quarters. Elsewhere in the city a color code indicates tl
restrictions. A red curb means no parking at all, green represents
10-minute parking limit, yellow is a loading zone, and a white cu
is a no-parking zone permitting passenger loading only. The to\
trucks mean business, especially if you block a fire hydrant or a b
stop. Read the posted signs on all streets for street cleaning days ar
other parking restrictions, including no parking rules on downtov
streets between 3 and 6pm.

Fuel. Most gas (petrol) stations are self-service and are equipped
accept credit cards for payment at the pump. "Full-serve" is mo
expensive, but it may include a window cleaning. Gas stations
open every day from early in the morning until 10pm or later.

Breakdowns and services. The American Automobile Associatic
(AAA) offers assistance to members of affiliated organizatior

110

abroad. It also provides travel information for the US and can arrange automobile insurance by the month for owner-drivers. In San Francisco the AAA-affiliated automobile club is the California State Automobile Association, 150 Van Ness Avenue; Tel. (415) 565-2012. In case of breakdown, dial (800) AAA-Help (toll-free) for information on how to obtain emergency assistance.

Fluid measures

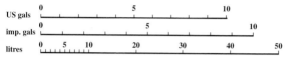

Distance

E

EARTHQUAKES

Basically, the Bay Area is in the line of fire. If you feel a tremor while you're indoors, stay there, preferably under a heavy table. Outdoors, avoid trees, power lines, and the walls of buildings. In a car, sit it out by the side of the road, but away from power lines and bridges. If you want to be prepared for the worst, study the San Francisco telephone directory, which contains four pages of earthquake instructions. If you'd like to find out what a tremor feels like, stop by the California Academy of Sciences and check out the earthquake exhibit.

ELECTRICITY

Throughout the United States the standard is 110 volts, 60 cycle AC. Plugs have two flat prongs. Overseas visitors without dual-voltage travel appliances will need a transformer and adapter plug for appliances such as an electric razor or a hair dryer.

EMBASSIES & CONSULATES

All embassies in the US are in Washington, DC, but some countrie
also maintain consulates in San Francisco. To find the address of
consulate, look in the alphabetical listings of the telephone director
under "Consulates" or in the *Yellow Pages* under "Consulates an
Other Foreign Government Representatives."

Australia: 1 Bush Street, Suite 1103; Tel. (415) 362-6160.

Canada: 300 S Grand Avenue, Los Angeles; Tel. (213) 346-2700.

Ireland: 44 Montgomery Street, Suite 3830; Tel. (415) 392-4214.

New Zealand: 1 Maritime Plaza; Tel. (415) 399-1255.

South Africa: 6300 Wilshire Blvd, Suite 600, Los Angeles 9004{
Tel. (323) 651-0902.

United Kingdom: 1 Sansome Street, Suite 850; Tel. (415) 981-303(

EMERGENCIES (see also HEALTH, MEDICAL CARE, & POLICE)

Call the all-purpose emergency number, 911, from any telephone; n
coins are required. The operator will note the information and rela
it to the police, ambulance, or the fire department, accordingly.

G

GAY & LESBIAN TRAVELERS

San Francisco is, arguably, the "gayest" city in the US. Most of th
scene is concentrated in the Castro neighborhood, but you will fir
gay places all over town. The *Bay Area Reporter* has the most con
prehensive listings and is available free. Most of the lesbian con
munity is centered around Valencia Street and Noe Valley.

GETTING THERE

By Air. Dozens of international flights serve San Francisco daily. Tł
major carriers offer non-stop flights from Europe to San Francisco, ‹
connections via New York, Chicago, or Los Angeles. There are noi
stop or one-stop flights from the principal Pacific airports. Beyond tł

standard first class, business/club, and economy fares, the principal cost-cutting possibilities are variations of APEX (book 21 days before departure for stays of 7 days to 6 months). Off-season reduced fares and package deals are also available. Certain US airlines offer bargains for foreign travelers who visit several American destinations.

From North America, direct flights connect American and Canadian cities to San Francisco. Special fares are available on these highly competitive routes and prices frequently change. Fly-drive vacations, including flight, hotel, and rental car, are offered by many airlines.

By Rail. Amtrak, the passenger railway company, goes only as far as Oakland, where special shuttle buses take passengers to the Ferry Building at Market and Embarcadero streets in San Francisco. The *California Zephyr* links Oakland with Chicago and Denver. The *Coast Starlight* stops in Oakland on the way from Portland and Seattle to Los Angeles and San Diego. Amtrak offers special package tours. Travelers who are permanent residents of countries outside the United States and Canada are eligible to buy USA Rail Passes covering 45 days of unlimited travel on Amtrak. If your travel agent lacks the information, write to Amtrak International Sales, 50 Massachusetts Avenue, NE, Washington, DC 20002. In the US, telephone (800) USA-RAIL (toll-free).

By Bus. Long-distance Greyhound-Trailways buses use the Transbay Terminal. For more information about bus services across the continent, telephone Greyhound-Trailways toll-free at (800) 231-2222.

By Car. The excellent Interstate freeway system criss-crosses all of the United States. Odd numbers designate freeways running north to south, while even-numbered interstates run east to west. Interstate 101, for instance, serves the length of California, entering San Francisco via the Golden Gate Bridge and leaving near the airport.

GUIDES & TOURS

San Francisco tour companies offer bus, boat, bike, and foot excursions aimed at the broadest or narrowest interest, from a one-hour glimpse of the city's highlights aboard a simulated cable car to walking (and eating and shopping) tour of Chinatown or the Castro. Leaflets listing the possibilities proliferate in hotel lobbies and the Visitor Information Center at Powell and Market streets. Some tour companies are geared to providing guides who speak foreign languages, but advance notice may be required. Bargain hunters and anyone interested in the history of San Francisco should contact City Guides (Tel. 415-557-4266) for information on their 35 free weekly walking tours.

H

HEALTH & MEDICAL CARE

Everywhere in the United States health care is extremely expensive, especially hospitalization, which can quickly become an economic disaster. It is essential, before you leave home, to sign up for medical insurance covering your stay. This can be arranged through an insurance company or agent or through your travel agent as part of a travel insurance package. Foreign visitors in need may wish to ask their consulate for a list of doctors.

Tap water is perfectly safe to drink everywhere in the Bay Area.

Drugstores (pharmacies). Many drugstores of the Walgreen chain stay open 24 hours a day; in others, pharmacists are available until midnight. Check with your hotel. You may find that some medicines obtainable over the counter in your home country are available only by prescription in the US, and vice versa.

HOLIDAYS

Banks, post offices, government buildings, and some businesses are closed on the following major holidays:

1 January	New Years Day
Third Monday in January	Martin Luther King Day
Third Monday in February	Presidents' Day
Last Monday in May	Memorial Day
4 July	Independence Day
First Monday in September	Labor Day
Second Monday in October	Columbus Day
11 November	Veterans' Day
Last Thursday in November	Thanksgiving
25 December	Christmas Day

I

INTERNET CAFÉS

You can check your email while on the road at The CoffeeNet, 744 Harrison Street (between 3rd and 4th streets), open for java and internet access Monday through Friday from 7am to 4:30pm; and Cafe.com, 970 Market Street (near Mason Street), open Monday through Saturday from 8am to 10pm.

L

LANGUAGE

American English is spoken here. Also Chinese, Japanese, Spanish, Russian, and many other languages — San Francisco is a cosmopolitan city.

LAUNDRY & DRY CLEANING

Express laundry and dry-cleaning services are available at most hotels, though this is expensive. If money is a factor, you can seek out a neighborhood laundry or cleaning establishment; same-day or even one-hour service may be offered. Laundromats (launderettes), self-service establishments with coin-operated washing machines and dryers, are a

cheaper alternative. One bold step beyond the laundromat is an establishment called Brain Wash at 1126 Folsom Street, which adds food,
drink, and music to the wash-and-dry formula; open until 11pm.

LIQUOR LAWS

Liquor is sold in supermarkets and even some drugstores, but not
between 2am and 6am. The same schedule restrictions affect restaurants and bars; some can serve only beer and wine. You may be asked
to prove you are 21, the legal age for drinking in California.

M

MAPS

Various cartographic companies publish detailed maps of San
Francisco which are sold at bookstores, news kiosks, and gas stations. A comprehensive map of the city's streets and public transport
system is sold by Muni, the San Francisco Municipal Railway. Free
tourist magazines usually include maps of the most popular areas.

MEDIA

The major daily newspaper in town is the *San Francisco
Chronicle*. Delivered in the morning, it is available from sidewalk
kiosks and often at your hotel's front desk. Almost every hotel
room has radio and television with a vast choice of programs.
Broadcasting is a round-the-clock business, and in San Francisco
that includes a wide range of foreign languages. The nationwide
commercial networks are found on channels 2, 4, 5, and 7, and
channel 9 is the local affiliate of Public Broadcasting Service
(PBS), with higher quality output as a rule, and commercial-free.
Most hotels have cable TV, which includes such programming as
CNN, the 24-hour news service.

On the radio, dial 810AM for news, weather and traffic reports.

MONEY

Currency. The dollar ($) is divided into 100 cents (¢).

Banknotes: $1, $5, $10, $20, $50, and $100. Larger denominations are not in general circulation. All notes are the same size and the same black-and-green color, so be sure to double-check your cash before you dispense it.

Coins: 1¢ (penny), 5¢ (nickel), 10¢ (dime), 25¢ (quarter), 50¢ (half dollar), and $1.

Banks and currency exchange. Banks are open from 9am to 5pm, Monday to Thursday, until 6pm Friday, and some operate on Saturday morning as well. You can change foreign currency at the airport, at leading banks downtown, and at bureaux de change in areas frequented by tourists or financiers.

Credit cards. When buying something or paying a restaurant bill you may be asked, "Cash or charge?" In the US "plastic" money is a way of life. Most Americans carry a variety of credit cards, and they are accepted in most places. But you may be asked for supplementary identification.

Traveler's checks. Banks, stores, restaurants, and hotels almost universally accept dollar-denominated traveler's checks as the equivalent of cash. It's straightforward if the checks are issued by American Express or an American bank, much less so if the issuer is not well known in the US. If your traveler's checks are in foreign denominations, they can be changed only in banks with experience in international transactions. Exchange only small amounts at a time, keeping the balance in your hotel safe if possible. Keep a record of the serial numbers in a separate place to facilitate a refund in the event of loss or theft.

Sales taxes. In the absence of VAT, cities and states around the US levy sales taxes and other hidden extras. An 8.5 percent sales tax is added to the price of all goods and services in San Francisco.

O

OPEN HOURS

Shops. Department stores are generally open from Monday to Saturday between 9:30 and 10am and stay in business until 6pm or, in some cases, as late as 8pm. They are often open on Sunday.

Museums. Hours vary, but 10am to 5pm is your best bet; Monday is the favorite closing day, and some also close on Tuesday.

Banks. Hours are generally from 9am to 4pm Monday to Friday, though some stay open longer.

Post offices. Branch post offices stay open from 8:30 or 9am to 5 or 5:30pm Monday to Friday; the General Post Office is open round the clock.

P

PLANNING YOUR TRIP on the WEB

These web sites are full of information to aid in getting a head start on your vacation.

www.bayarea.citysearch.com A comprehensive, regularly updated site devoted to all things San Francisco including arts, entertainment, dining, and attractions with links to the hotel reservation network.

www.sfbg.com The San Francisco Bay Guardian site with event listings and the low-down on nightlife.

www.sfgate.com The *San Francisco Chronicle* web site. Read all about it.

www.qsanfrancisco.com A web site for gay and lesbian travelers.

POLICE

The blue-uniformed city police, some of them multilingual, are courteous and helpful to tourists. Imitating a feature of Japanese life, they operate *kobans* or mini police stations at Market and Powell streets; in Chinatown on Grant Avenue between Washington and Jackson streets; and in Japantown at Post and Buchanan streets. Out of town on roads, you'll encounter the California Highway Patrol in tan uniforms with ranger hats. In an emergency dial **911.**

POST OFFICES

The US postal service deals only with mail. The main post office is at Seventh Street and Mission Street. A branch post office in the basement of Macy's department store, Union Square, is convenient.

PUBLIC TRANSPORTATION

Muni Metro **streetcars** operate underground in the downtown district, above ground beyond the center. There are five lines, making the same Market Street stops as the BART system. Board buses through the front door and leave from the rear. The exact fare is required; drivers don't give change. The problem is avoided if you buy a Muni Passport valid for a full day (or three days or a week) on all lines, including the cable cars. The passes, on sale at the Visitor Information Center (see page 122) and other locations, also provide discounts to museums and other attractions.

Cable cars, on three lines, go over the hills to the principal areas of tourist interest. Tickets are sold on board and drivers will make change. The cable cars are usually crowded, mostly with tourists enjoying the invigorating ride. Never board or leave a cable car until it has stopped; get off facing the direction of travel.

BART, the pioneering Bay Area Rapid Transit system, offers fast, quiet, comfortable rail service between San Francisco and 25 stations in the East Bay area (Oakland, Richmond, and so forth). Maps and charts in the stations explain the routes and the computerized ticketing system. There are change-giving machines alongside the coin-operated ticket dispensing machines.

San Francisco

Intercity buses operate from the Transbay Terminal, at First and Mission streets. AC Transit crosses the Bay Bridge to Berkeley, Oakland, and other East Bay communities. Golden Gate Transit uses the Golden Gate Bridge to serve Marin and Sonoma Counties. Samtrans is the San Mateo County service, going as far as Palo Alto.

Taxis are usually plentiful. They congregate at the luxury hotels but you can hail one in the street. If you're staying at an out-of-the-way location, it's convenient to telephone for a radio-dispatched taxi.

Ferry boats seemed to be doomed when the bridges were built but today they once more provide commuter service and useful tourist travel. The principal terminals are the Ferry Building, at the foot of Market Street, and Piers 39 to 41/2. The Blue & Gold Fleet, which does big business in Bay sightseeing cruises, also goes to Oakland, Alameda, and Alcatraz. Golden Gate Ferries go to Sausalito and Larkspur. The Red & White Fleet cruises to Sausalito, Tiburon, and Vallejo.

RELIGION

Every imaginable religious denomination has a house of worship in San Francisco, and services are available in many languages. The Saturday newspapers list times of some of the services. The Visitor Information Center (see page 122) has a list of church addresses, or ask at your hotel. For a rousing, gospel music-filled Sunday service that reflects the city's multiculturalism, show up a half-hour before the 9am or 11am celebration at Glide Memorial Church, 330 Ellis Street (Tel. 415-771-6300).

SMOKING

Smoking is prohibited in public places such as office buildings, schools, libraries, public rest rooms, and service or check-out lines.

In liberal San Francisco, it's even banned in bars and restaurants. Domestic airlines prohibit smoking on-board planes, even on the long transcontinental flights.

TELEPHONE

The American telephone system is run by private, regional companies. Coin- or card-operated phones are found in all public places — hotel lobbies, drugstores, gas stations, bars, restaurants, and along the streets. Directions for use are clearly stated on the machine. For local directory assistance dial 555-1212 (free of charge). When calling long distance, the rules of competition mean that you often have to choose between companies by pushing one or another button; to the visitor it scarcely matters which. Evening (after 5pm) and weekend rates are much cheaper. Many hotels, airlines, and business firms have toll free numbers (beginning 800, 888, or 877) so you can avoid long-distance charges.

Some hotels add a hefty surcharge to their guests' outgoing calls, local or long-distance. If it seems exorbitant you can go out to use a pay phone. But you'll have to have a hoard of coins at the ready; an electronic voice may break in to tell you to insert more. However, phone cards and sometimes credit cards may now also be used for dialing telephone calls.

The long distance code for the city of San Francisco is 415. The code for most of the East Bay area, including Oakland and Berkeley, is 510.

TIME ZONES

The continental United States is divided into four time zones. San Francisco is in the Pacific zone, which is 8 hours behind GMT. Between the first Sunday in April and the last Sunday in October, the clock is advanced 1 hour for Daylight Saving Time (GMT minus 7 hours). These dates are not quite synchronized with the changes in other countries. The following chart shows the time in various cities when it is noon in San Francisco.

San Francisco

Note that Americans customarily write dates in a different order from the day/month/year system of Europe. Thus the US 1/17/00 means 17 January 2000.

San Francisco noon	Chicago 2pm	New York 3pm	London 8pm	Paris 9pm

TIPPING

You are expected to add about 15 percent to restaurant and bar bills, based on the total of the bill. If service has been exceptionally good, 20 percent is appropriate. Even in informal coffee shops, some coins are often left on the table or counter. Cinema or theater ushers are not tipped, but doormen, cloakroom attendants, etc., should be remunerated — no less than 50 cents. Some general guidelines:

Bartender	$1 per round of drinks
Porter	$1 per bag
Hotel maid	$1 per day (except for very short stays)
Lavatory attendant	50¢
Taxi driver	about 15%
Tour guide	10-15%
Hairdresser/barber	15%

TOILETS

Some dark-green coin-operated public bathrooms are located near tourist sites on Market Street and Fisherman's Wharf. Many restaurants discourage anyone but patrons from using their facilities; your best bet is to try a department store, hotel, or gas station, where you may have to ask for the key.

TOURIST INFORMATION

For advance inquiries, write to the San Francisco Convention & Visitors Bureau, 201 Third Street, Suite 900, San Francisco, CA 94103. The bureau publishes a 96-page information brochure, *The*

San Francisco Book, available at a cost of $3 to cover postage and handling. You could also contact the US Embassy, Visit USA Committee, or USTTA (United States Travel and Tourism Administration) in your own country:

Australia: Suite 6106, MLC Center, King and Castlereagh Streets, Sydney, New South Wales 2000; Tel. (612) 233 4666

Canada: 800 Rochester Boulevard, West Suite 1110, Montreal, Quebec H3B 1X9; Tel. (514) 861 5036

Ireland: Irish Visit USA Committee, c/o Tour America, 62 Middle Abbey St., Dublin; Tel. (353) (1) 662-0860.

New Zealand: Visit USA Commitee, 129A Kohimarama Road, Kohimarama, Auckland; Tel. (64) (9) 528 4447.

South Africa: US Embassy, P.O. Box 9536, Pretoria 0001; Tel. (271) (2) 342-1048

UK: 22 Sackville Street, London W1X 2EA; Tel. 071 439 7433

In San Francisco, the Visitor Information Center is located on the lower level of Hallidie Plaza at Market and Powell streets, near the cable car terminus. The office is open weekdays from 9am to 5:30pm, Saturday and Sunday from 9am to 3pm. Telephone inquiries: (415) 391-2000. A recorded message listing daily events is available on (415) 391-2001. (In French, 415-391-2003; German, 415-391-2004; Spanish, 415-391-2122; Japanese, 415-391-2101.)

WEIGHTS & MEASURES

Efforts to ease the United States into the metric system are proceeding slowly. The government itself is said to be converting to international measurements, and indeed the national parks use kilometers (to the bafflement of most of their visitors), but in real life it's still inches, feet, yards, miles, and degrees Fahrenheit.

San Francisco

Length

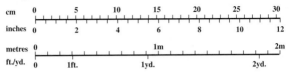

Weight

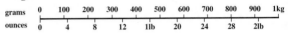

Temperature

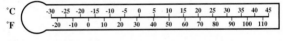

YOUTH HOSTELS

The Golden Gate Council of American Youth Hostels operates budget accommodation at Union Square and Fort Mason as well as hostels in scenic locations around the Bay area. The address of the Union Square installation, with lodgings for 175 people, is 312 Mason Street, San Francisco, CA 94102; Tel. (415) 788-5604. You can contact the Fort Mason Hostel, capacity 150, at Building 240, Fort Mason, San Francisco, CA 94123; Tel. (415) 771-7277. In Sausalito, you can try the Golden Gate Youth Hostel, 941 Fort Barry, Sausalito, CA 94965; Tel. (415) 331-2777. Additional hostels are listed in the Lodging Guide issued by the San Francisco Convention & Visitors Bureau (see page 122).

Note that advance booking is essential at all Youth Hostels in San Francisco. For more information, contact: the American Youth Hostels Inc, National Offices, PO Box 37613, Washington, DC 20013–7613; Tel. (202) 783-6171.

Recommended Hotels

San Francisco holds a dizzying array of hotels, motels, Bed & Breakfasts, and inns that range from dull to dramatic. All the major chains are well represented, but the more interesting rooms are located in "boutique" hotels. These are small properties developed around a theme, such as books, rock and roll, or the movies, that gives the hotel some definable personality.

Whether a boutique, a B&B, or a 1,000-room behemoth that will honor your frequent flier mileage, all the hotels listed below are well-scrubbed and offer excellent service. Rooms will generally include cable television and direct-dial telephones, but not air-conditioning (it isn't really necessary). If there is no concierge, desk clerks will do their best to provide information and make tour and restaurant reservations. Since San Francisco is a very popular convention and tourist town, it is imperative to make reservations well ahead of time. If you haven't done so, phone SF Reservations, Tel. (800) 667-1500 (toll-free in US) or 415-227-1500 or California Reservations, Tel. (415) 252-1107.

The stars below refer to high-season rack rates for a standard double room, exclusive of taxes (14 percent). Prices do not include parking or breakfast unless noted. When making reservations at the larger hotels, always inquire about special packages and discounts. Toll-free numbers are effective only within North America.

The following symbols apply for a double room:

$$$$$	above $250
$$$$	$200–$250
$$$	$150–$200
$$	$125–$150
$	below $125

San Francisco

UNION SQUARE

Andrews Hotel $$ *624 Post Street, SF 94108; Tel. (415) 563-6877; (800) 926-3739 (toll-free in US); fax (415) 928-6919; web site <www.andrewshotel.com>*. A 1905 Victorian well-located two blocks west of Union Square. The rooms and baths are on the small side, but rates include a continental breakfast and evening wine reception. No concierge, room service. Smoking is not allowed. 48 rooms. Major credit cards.

Campton Place Hotel $$$$$ *340 Stockton Street, SF 94108; Tel. (415) 781-5555; (800) 235-4300 (toll-free in US); fax (415) 955-5536; web site <www.camptonplace.com>*. Elegant, luxurious, and intimate, this is one of the most renowned and refined hotels in the city. The service is excellent, the amenities, which include assistance unpacking and daily papers, are top-notch, and the hotel restaurant consistently merits top ratings. Wheelchair accessible. 110 rooms. Major credit cards.

Cartwright Hotel $$–$$$ *524 Sutter Street, SF 94102; Tel. (415) 421-2865; (800) 227-3844 (toll-free in US); fax (415) 983-6244; web site <www.cartwrighthotel.com>*. This genteel hotel has tastefully decorated rooms with handsome antiques and many amenities, including bathrobes and irons. A continental breakfast and afternoon tea are included in the rates. Five suites are available, a plus for families, and two floors are reserved for smokers. Be sure to ask about specials. 114 rooms. Major credit cards.

Chancellor Hotel $$ *433 Powell Street, SF 94102; Tel. (415) 362-2004; (800) 428-4748 (toll-free in US); fax (415) 362-1403; web site <www.chancellorhotel.com>*. The same family has owned and managed this charming hotel since 1917, which is on the Powell Street cable car line and within a stone's throw of the major department stores around Union Square. Rooms are brightly decorated and comfortably furnished; baths are small but well-stocked. 137 rooms. Major credit cards.

Commodore International $–$$ *825 Sutter Street, SF 94109; Tel. (415) 923-6800; (800) 338-6848 (toll-free in US); fax (415) 923-6804; web site <www.sftrips.com>.* Spacious rooms with large baths are bright and recently renovated in a nautical theme. Three blocks from Union Square, the location is a bit close to the seedy Tenderloin neighborhood for some, but that's why rates are low. A café sits on one side of the property and a trendy bar is on the other. 113 rooms. Major credit cards.

Golden Gate Hotel $ *775 Bush Street, SF 94108; Tel. (415) 392-3702; (800) 835-1118 (toll-free in US); fax (415) 392-6202; web site <www.goldengatehotel.com>.* A cozy family-run hotel in an old Edwardian near Union Square and two blocks from the Chinatown Gate. The small, pretty rooms contain few amenities, but rates include a continental breakfast and afternoon tea. Excellent location for walkers and cable car fans. Smoking is not allowed in the hotel. 25 rooms, 14 with private bath. Major credit cards.

Handlery Union Square Hotel $$$ *351 Geary Street, SF 94102; Tel. (415) 781-7800, (800) 843-4343 (toll-free in US); fax (415) 781-0269; web site <www.handlerysf@handlery.com>.* A good choice for families, the hotel has a heated pool, morning and evening room service, even Nintendo games. Club rooms, located in an adjacent building, are large and offer dressing areas, robes, newspapers, and fresh decor. Two-bedroom suites are also available. Wheelchair accessible. 379 rooms. Major credit cards.

San Francisco

The Inn at Union Square $$$–$$$$$ *440 Post Street, SF 94102; Tel. (415) 397-3510; (800) 288-4346 (toll-free in US); fax (415) 989-0529; web site <www.unionsquare.com>.* Furnished with Georgian antiques, this is a "European-style" inn with excellent service and a no-tipping policy. Extras include a complimentary continental breakfast, afternoon tea, fresh flowers, newspapers, and concierge. The larger rooms have fireplaces. Smoking, however, is not allowed in the hotel. Wheelchair accessible. 30 rooms. Major credit cards.

The Juliana $$$ *590 Bush Street, SF 94108; Tel. (415) 392-2540; (800) 328-3880 (toll-free in US); fax (415) 391-8447; web site <www.julianahotel.com>.* Situated between Nob Hill and Union Square, the Juliana is a cozy retreat with gaily decorated rooms and suites that include coffee pots, irons, and hair dryers. Baths are small. An evening wine reception is hosted nightly in front of the fireplace; continental breakfast is available for an extra charge. 107 rooms. Major credit cards.

Kensington Park Hotel $$$ *450 Post Street, SF 94102; Tel. (415) 788-6400; (800) 553-1900 (toll-free in US); fax (415) 399-9484; web site <www.personalityhotels.com>.* Larger-than-average recently renovated rooms and baths distinguish this fine hotel, which is next door to a trendy seafood restaurant and shares space with a live theater. Rates include continental breakfast and afternoon tea; concierge services are friendly and helpful. 86 rooms. Major credit cards.

King George Hotel $$–$$$ *334 Mason Street, SF 94102; Tel. (415) 781-5050; (800) 288-6005 (toll-free in US).* Opened in 1913, this is a British-themed hotel with really small rooms and baths updated in 1998. Friendly staff and 24-hour room service, plus a tea room presided over by a handsome portrait of Queen Elizabeth. Continental breakfast and afternoon tea are served daily, but aren't included in the rates. 143 rooms. Major credit cards.

The Maxwell $$$–$$$$ *386 Geary Street, SF 94102; Tel. (415) 986-2000; (800) 821-5343 (toll-free in US); fax (415) 397-2447; web site <www.sftrips.com>.* An inviting, theatrical lobby leads to Art-Deco–inspired guestrooms that range from small to spacious. Amenities include a newsletter highlighting shopping opportunities around the city. Max's on the Square offers room service from 7am to 10pm and desk staff provide concierge services. 152 rooms. Major credit cards.

Hotel Monaco $$$$ *501 Geary Street, SF 94102; Tel. (415) 292-0100; (800) 214-4220 (toll-free in US); fax (415) 292-0111; web site <www.hotelmonaco.com>.* Rooms in this hotel are comfortable and plush, featuring lots of wallpaper, patterns, canopied beds, and modern furniture with a 1920s-inspired twist. The hotel serves mostly a largely corporate clientele, so expect to find major amenities including a fitness room. The excellent Grand Café is next door and provides 24-hour room service. Wheelchair accessible. 201 rooms. Major credit cards.

Petite Auberge $$–$$$ *863 Bush Street, SF 94102; Tel. (415) 928-6000; (800) 365-3004 (toll-free in US); fax (415) 775-5717; web site <www.foursisters.com>.* Full of floral patterns and French country accents, this is a most romantic B&B. A full breakfast is served in a homey dining room as well as complimentary afternoon tea and wine. The less expensive rooms have showers only; the high-end rooms are large with full baths, and all are very comfortable. Book way ahead of time. 26 rooms. Major credit cards.

San Francisco

Hotel Rex $$$–$$$$$ *562 Sutter Street, SF 94102; Tel. (415) 433-4434; (800) 433-4434 (toll-free in US); fax (415) 433-3695; web site <sftrips.com>.* With a nod to the 1930s, the sophisticated Rex is a favorite among the literati. There's even an antiquarian bookstore on the premises. Rooms range from smallish doubles to large kings and all are smartly designed with amenities including CD players. An evening wine hour is complimentary; a continental breakfast is available at an additional charge. 94 rooms. Major credit cards.

The Ritz-Carlton, San Francisco $$$$$ *600 Stockton Street, SF 94108; Tel. (415) 296-7465; (800) 241-3333 (toll-free in US); fax (415) 291-0288; web site <www.ritzcarlton.com>.* Once a giant neo-classical corporate headquarters, now a luxury hotel catering to deep pocketbooks. Opened in 1991, the Ritz offers enormous rooms, a fitness center, indoor pool, fine dining restaurant, and primo service. Wheelchair accessible. 336 rooms. Major credit cards.

Sir Francis Drake $$$–$$$$$ *450 Powell Street, SF 94102; Tel. (415) 392-7755; (800) 652-1668 (toll-free in US); fax (415) 391-8719; web site <www.sirfrancisdrake.com>.* Glide past the uniformed valets into the grand lobby of this 1928 landmark building. Newly renovated, the rooms are pretty and offer lots of upscale amenities. The excellent Scala's Bistro is located next door and there's a small fitness room and popular nightclub on the premises. Wheelchair accessible. 417 rooms. Major credit cards.

Hotel Triton $$$–$$$$ *342 Grant Avenue, SF 94108; Tel. (415) 394-0500; (800) 433-6611 (toll-free in US); fax (415) 394-0555; web site <www.hotel-tritonsf.com>.* Rock music greets patrons entering this trendy hotel just across the street from the Chinatown Dragon Gate. The wild designs and mod furniture scattered around the lobby are amusing, but don't completely compensate for the tiny bedrooms. Lots of amenities, including robes, hair dryers, concierge, Nintendo and an itty bitty fitness room. 147 rooms. Major credit cards.

Warwick Regis $$-$$$ *490 Geary Street, SF 94102; Tel. (415) 928-7900; (800) 827-3447 (toll-free in US); fax (415) 441-8788; web site <www.warwickhotels.com>.* Guests receive all the amenities expected of a much larger hotel — twice-daily maid service, fresh flowers, marble-tiled baths, and 24-hour room service — for a relatively modest tariff. Twelve of the suites contain two baths; all the elegantly appointed guestrooms are quiet. The Union Square location is especially convenient for theater-goers. 74 rooms. Major credit cards.

Westin St. Francis $$$$ *335 Powell Street, SF 94102; Tel. (415) 397-7000; (800) 228-3000 (toll-free in US); fax (415) 774-0124.* The location, across the street from Union Square, adds to the excitement of staying at this legendary hotel. If the historic aspects interest you, reserve a room in the original building. Baths are small and guest rooms rather dark, but they're furnished with handsome reproductions and chandeliers. On-site fitness center, room service, and restaurants complete the package. Wheelchair accessible. 1,192 rooms. Major credit cards.

NOB HILL

Huntington Hotel $$$$$ *1075 California Street, SF 94108; Tel. (415) 474-5400; (800) 227-4683 (toll-free in US); fax (415) 474-6227; web site <www.slh.com>.* A refined family-owned hotel built in 1924 at the top of Nob Hill, where publicity-shy celebrities stay in discreet luxury. Originally an apartment building, rooms are larger than average although baths are small. For views, ask for a room above the eighth floor. A park and playground is located across the street, making the location especially pleasant for families with young children. Wheelchair accessible. 140 rooms. Major credit cards.

Mark Hopkins Inter-Continental $$$$$ *999 California, SF 94108; Tel. (415) 392-3434; (800) 327-0200 (toll-free in US).* At the summit of Nob Hill, with grand views in all directions, this hotel offers totally redecorated luxury rooms on the site of the original Mark Hopkins mansion. The rooftop cocktail lounge, Top of the Mark, has been a city tradition since 1939, and an atmosphere of quiet refinement prevails throughout. Wheelchair accessible. 392 rooms. Major credit cards.

Nob Hill Lambourne $$$$–$$$$$ *725 Pine Street, SF 94108; Tel. (415) 433-2287; (800) 274-8466 (toll-free in US); fax (415) 433-0975; web site <www.sftrips.com>.* Intimate and soothing, you'll find lovely spacious guestrooms with compact kitchenettes and many amenities. Desk staff acts as concierge and can schedule on-site massages and spa treatments. A continental breakfast is included in the rates; smoking is not allowed inside the premises. 20 rooms. Major credit cards.

THE EMBARCADERO

Embarcadero Hyatt $$$–$$$$$ *5 Market Street, SF 94105; Tel. (415) 788-1234; toll-free (800) 233-1234; fax (415) 398-2567; web site <www.sanfrancisco.regency.hyatt.com>.* This is one of those enormous chain hotels where it's possible to get lost on the way to one's room, but the location at the foot of Market Street is splendid for walkers and public transportation users. Some great restaurants are close by as well. Big rooms, on-site fitness center, the works. Wheelchair accessible. 804 rooms. Major credit cards.

Harbor Court Hotel $$$$ *165 Steuart Street, SF 94105; tel.(415) 882-1300; (800) 346-0555 (toll-free in US); fax (415) 882-1313; web site <www.harborcourthotel.com>*. Across from the Rincon Center, this 1907 building with spectacular bay views has been converted into a "European-style" hotel with large, comfortable rooms and varied luxury amenities. Guests have complimentary access to the state-of-the-art YMCA located next door. Wheelchair accessible. 131 rooms. Major credit cards.

SOMA

Hotel Milano $$$–$$$$ *55 Fifth Street, SF, 94103; Tel. (415) 543-8555; (800) 398-7555 (toll-free in US); fax (415) 543-5885; web site <www.hotelmilano.citysearch.com>*. The location off Market Street — next door to the San Francisco Centre, a few blocks from Yerba Buena Gardens, and close to an underground Muni station — makes this hotel a good pick for energetic tourists who like to shop. An on-site fitness room, restaurant, and full service make up for the spare decor. Wheelchair accessible. 108 rooms. Major credit cards.

MARINA

Hotel Del Sol $$ *3100 Webster Street, SF 94123; Tel. (415) 921-5520; (877) 433-5765 (toll-free in US); fax (415) 931-4137; web site <www.sftrips.com>*. Once a boring, ordinary motel, the Del Sol proves that looks are almost everything. Color is the watchword here, splashed on walls, fabrics, and mosaic tiles that decorate tabletops and walkways. Comfortable medium- to large-sized rooms surround a heated pool, small lawn and hammock; suites are available, and parking is free. Wheelchair accessible. 57 rooms. Major credit cards.

The Marina Inn $ *3110 Octavia, SF 94123; Tel. (415) 928-1000; (800) 274-1420 (toll-free in US); fax (415) 928-5909; web site <www.marinainn.com>.* This is an inexpensive, gracious Victorian inn off Lombard Street, close to the Golden Gate Bridge, the Presidio, and upscale shopping on Union and Chestnut Streets. Rooms are simply furnished with wooden beds and armoires; inside rooms are quieter but don't have much natural light. No concierge. Complimentary continental breakfast. Wheelchair accessible. 40 rooms. Major credit cards.

NORTH BEACH/FISHERMAN'S WHARF

Hotel Bohème $$ *444 Columbus Street, SF 94133; Tel. (415) 433-9111; fax (415) 362-6292; web site <www.hotel boheme.com>.* A flight of narrow stairs brings you inside this delightful small hotel in the heart of North Beach. Iron beds and brightly painted walls grace the small but lovely bedrooms, and the baths are well-stocked. No concierge, but the front desk will assist with rental cars, dinner reservations, and tours. 15 rooms. Major credit cards.

Tuscan Inn $$$ *425 North Point, SF 94133; Tel. (415) 561-1100; (800) 648-4626 (toll-free in US); fax (415) 561-1199; web site <www.tuscaninn.com>.* Of the many hotels around Fisherman's Wharf, this is by far the most palatable. The concierge is enthusiastic and helpful, the attractive rooms are well-sized by local standards, and the location is appealing to families who wish, for whatever reason, to be near Pier 39. Wheelchair accessible. 221 rooms. Major credit cards.

Recommended Restaurants

With over 3,300 restaurants in the city limits, there are many worthy dining establishments from which to choose; the ones below provide a representative sample of neighborhoods, styles of cuisine, and prices. Always phone ahead for dinner reservations; you're competing with San Francisco's resident population of gourmets, who have made table-hopping an art form. The following three price categories apply for a three-course meal without wine:

$$$	Over $40
$$	$20–$40
$	under $20

Remember, taxes (8.5 percent) and tips (15 percent) will also increase your bill.

CHINATOWN

Kay Cheung $ *615 Jackson Street; Tel. (415) 989-6838.* Open daily for dim sum, lunch and dinner. This small, pleasant dining room serves delicious Hong Kong–style Chinese dishes at a great price. Interesting selection of fresh seafood (plucked live from tanks) and dim sum. If you end up sharing a table, take an opportunity to learn about dumplings from the Chinatown regulars who come here in-between shopping excursions. Major credit cards.

R&G Lounge $ *631 Kearney Street; Tel. (415) 982-7877.* Open for lunch and dinner daily. Downstairs you'll find excellent Hong Kong Chinese food served in a drab setting by bored waiters. The upstairs dining room is much more comfortable with attentive servers who can help design your meal. No matter where they seat you, don't pass up the live spot shrimp cooked two ways. Major credit cards.

UNION SQUARE

Dottie's True Blue Café $ *522 Jones Street; Tel. (415) 885-2767.* Open for breakfast and lunch Wednesday through Sunday only. If you like a big breakfast featuring fresh baked goods, pancakes, omelets, and maybe a pork chop, get in line for one of the 11 tables packed into this tiny place. Lunch isn't quite as crowded, but it's equally good. Major credit cards.

Grand Café $$ *501 Geary Street; Tel. (415) 292-0101.* Open daily for breakfast, lunch, and dinner. There's always a buzz of activity inside this vast muralled restaurant. It's a destination for tourists as well as locals looking for a major meal or just an after-theater bite. Roasts, fresh fish, brick-oven pizzas, big desserts — every plate receives careful attention from the kitchen. Major credit cards.

Le Colonial $$$ *20 Cosmo Place; Tel. (415) 931-3600.* Open weekdays for lunch; dinner nightly. Flavorful French-Vietnamese food is formally proffered in a dining room replete with rattan, pressed tin, potted palms, and ceiling fans. The upstairs lounge is a great place for a drink and to listen to live jazz on Friday and Sunday nights. Major credit cards.

Scala's Bistro $$ *432 Powell Street; Tel. (415) 395-8555.* Open daily for breakfast, lunch, and dinner. Next to the Sir Francis Drake hotel, this Italian restaurant has a broad menu, comfortable booths, and a warm, clubby atmosphere. Highlights include a terrific Caesar salad and well-prepared fish. Major credit cards.

NOB HILL

Charles Nob Hill $$$ *1250 Jones Street; Tel. (415) 771-5400.* Open for dinner only, Tuesday through Sunday. Ron Siegal, the resident kitchen god at this elegant and refined restaurant, is renowned in culinary circles for taking on Japan television's *Iron Chef* — and winning. His contemporary American cuisine is exquisitely prepared and presented with a slight French flair. The short rib ravioli underneath a perfect filet mignon is an especially magnificent dish. Major credit cards.

EMBARCADERO/FINANCIAL DISTRICT

Kokkari $$$ *200 Jackson Street; Tel. (415) 981-0983.* Open weekdays for lunch; dinner Monday through Saturday. An Aristotle Onassis–sort of Greek taverna with beamed ceilings, a massive fireplace, Oriental carpets, and huge dishes of rich food. (Don't expect to see anyone intentionally smash a plate.) The crowd exudes a robust sense of well-being. Reservations are advised. Major credit cards.

Plouf $$ *40 Belden Place; Tel. (415) 986-6491.* Open for lunch and dinner Monday through Saturday. There are a number of good cafés with outdoor seating on Belden Place, an alley off Bush and Kearney streets near the Financial District. Plouf specializes in delicious seafood prepared with a French affect and the waiters also give the impression you've arrived in the Paris of the west. Major credit cards.

Tadich Grill $$ *240 California Street; Tel. (415) 391-2373.* Open for lunch and dinner Monday through Saturday. This the oldest continually operating restaurant in California, with wooden booths, white linen, and waiters as crusty as the sourdough.

The menu of classics, including lobster Newburg, is printed daily. The cognoscenti order whatever fresh fish is available, grilled. Major credit cards.

SOMA

Hawthorne Lane $$$ *22 Hawthorne Lane (at Howard); Tel. (415) 777-9779.* Open for lunch weekdays and dinner nightly. The chefs who opened Postrio departed a few years back to open their own fine-dining establishment with a California/Asian-influenced cuisine. The art-filled setting and the food (for example, roasted local lamb with garlic chive risotto and a warm snap pea and water chestnut salad) are quite elegant, but overall it's warm and accessible. Major credit cards.

Thirsty Bear Brewing Company $$ *661 Howard Street; Tel. (415) 974-0905.* Open for lunch Monday through Saturday; dinner nightly. Excellent house-made beers and outstanding Catalan food have made this spot a favorite. The fish cheeks are one of the great *tapas* offered, but save room for a Sagrada Familia, two upside-down wafer cones filled with chocolate mousse and decorated with whipped cream. Major credit cards.

NORTH BEACH

Enrico's Sidewalk Café $$ *504 Broadway; Tel. (415) 982-6223.* Open for lunch and dinner daily. It's always fun to dine on the patio here and watch the action along busy and bawdy Broadway. Along with a seasonal menu of California cuisine, there's live jazz and a convivial atmosphere. Major credit cards.

L'Osteria del Forna $ *519 Columbus Avenue; Tel. (415) 982-1124.* Open for lunch and dinner Wednesday through Monday. For casual but satisfying Italian food including marvelous antipasti, thin-crusted pizzas, a daily pasta dish, and a fine roast pork loin simmered in a milky broth. A kid pleaser as well. Cash only.

CIVIC CENTER/HAYES VALLEY

Hayes Street Grill $$ *320 Hayes Street; Tel. (415) 863-5545.* Open for lunch weekdays; dinner nightly. Practically a local institution, this restaurant features fresh seafood prepared simply, with integrity, and served with terrific french fries. Non-fish items, such as a juicy hamburger, are also wonderful. Local politicians eat lunch here; the pre-symphony, opera, and ballet crowd fill the tables before 8pm. Major credit cards.

Zuni Café $$$ *1658 Market Street (Civic Center); Tel. (415) 552-2522.* Open for lunch Tuesday through Saturday; dinner Tuesday through Sunday; Sunday brunch. Make reservations and elbow your way past the crowded copper bar for the best roasted chicken and bread salad for two imaginable. Actually, everything on the California-cuisine based menu is going to be great. Major credit cards.

CASTRO

Chow $ *215 Church Street; Tel. (415) 552-2469.* Open daily for lunch and dinner. For casual but well-prepared meals that will appeal to children and grown-ups, make your way to this popular place or their equally busy restaurant on 9th Avenue by Golden Gate Park. Terrific pizzas, salads, sandwiches, brick-oven roasted chicken, and daily specials at prices that'll amaze you. Major credit cards.

JAPANTOWN

Café Kati $$$ *1963 Sutter Street; Tel. (415) 775-7313.* Open for dinner Tuesday through Sunday. Another outstanding neighborhood restaurant with a legion of loyal followers, this is well worth a cab ride out of Union Square. Major credit cards.

Mifune $ *1737 Post Street; Tel. (415) 922-0337*. The San Francisco branch of a famous Osaka restaurant proposes Japanese *udon* and *soba* in all their forms, often in steaming soups. This is the place for a quick lunch or dinner, and kids are very happy in the midst of all these noodles. Major credit cards.

MARINA

Greens $$ *Building A, Fort Mason; Tel. (415) 771-6222*. Open for lunch Tuesday through Saturday, dinner Monday through Saturday, and Sunday brunch. In a one-time army warehouse on the bay, an airy up-market vegetarian restaurant that even carnivores rave about. The Saturday evening prix fixe is a relative bargain and comes with lovely bay views. Reservations are essential. Major credit cards.

THE MISSION DISTRICT

Delfina $$ *3621 18th Street; Tel. (415) 552-4055*. Open nightly for dinner. The kitchen in this storefront restaurant turns out delicious Tuscan Italian food that provides a star turn for local, seasonal produce, fish, and meat. (If sea bass happens to be on the menu, catch it.) Reservations are essential as this is a favorite neighborhood pick among residents from all over the city. Major credit cards.

Slanted Door $$ *584 Valencia Street; Tel. (415) 861-8032*. Open for lunch and dinner Tuesday through Sunday. Classy Vietnamese dishes served in hip surroundings on a hot culinary island in the Mission. Caramelized chicken, "shaking" beef, and a sweet, buttery steamed sea bass are among the menu's delights. Reservations are a must for dinner. Major credit cards.

OUTSIDE THE CITY OF SAN FRANCISCO

Oakland

Bay Wolf Café $$–$$$ *3853 Piedmont Avenue, Oakland; Tel. (510) 655-6004*. Open for lunch Monday through Friday and dinner nightly. A pioneer of California-style nouvelle cuisine maintains enviable quality. Keenly chosen wine list. Major credit cards.

Yoshi's $$ *510 Embarcadero West, Jack London Square, Oakland; Tel. (510) 238-9200*. Open daily for lunch and dinner. The large, brightly lit restaurant serves good, if predictable, Japanese food and has a lively sushi bar. Diners receive priority seating in the well-known jazz club. Major credit cards.

Berkeley

Chez Panisse $$–$$$ *1517 Shattuck Avenue, Berkeley; Tel. (510) 548-5525*. Open Monday through Saturday for dinner; the café is also open for lunch. A redwood cottage is the shrine for spectacularly tasty and original California cuisine. The upstairs café, which does not require reservations, is less expensive than the downstairs dining room for which reservations are essential. Major credit cards.

Marin

Guaymas $$–$$$ *5 Main Street, Tiburon; Tel. (415) 435-6300*. Open daily for lunch and dinner. Modern Mexican decor and cuisine combines with panoramas of San Francisco. A major hangout for tourists. Major credit cards.

Lark Creek Inn $$$ *234 Magnolia Avenue, Larkspur; Tel. (415) 924-7766.* Open for lunch weekdays, dinner nightly, Sunday brunch. Set among a few redwoods in the pretty town of Larkspur, you'll be treated to top-notch American cuisine from the best hamburger in the state to a smoky, sun-dried tomato and ham hock–filled ravoli. Great children's menu. Reservations advised. Major credit cards.

Wine Country

Bistro Jeanty $$ *6510 Washington Street, Yountville; Tel. (707) 944-0103.* Open for lunch and dinner daily. A fairly new, very French bistro with an outdoor patio and spirited inside dining room and bar. The seasonal menu of homey dishes (coq au vin, rabbit and sweetbread ragout, cassoulet, a simple steak frites) is so satisfying you want to eat here again and again. Major credit cards.

Heirloom $$ *110 West Spain Street, Sonoma; Tel. (707) 939-6955.* Open daily for lunch and dinner. Inside the recently renovated Sonoma Hotel, take a seat in the secluded patio on a warm afternoon or inside the rustic dining room and prepare yourself for huge plates of local fare. You can never go wrong with the grilled rack of lamb. Major credit cards.

Tra Vigne $$ *1050 Charter Oak Avenue, St. Helena; Tel. (707) 963-4444.* Open daily for lunch and dinner. A large airy dining room opens onto a vine-filled patio with formidable stone tables and a whimsical fountain. The Italian fare is based on what's currently in the markets, and if it's tomato season, don't miss the fruits paired with fresh mozzarella. A delicatessen, the Cantinetta, offers prepared foods for picnicking. Major credit cards.

INDEX